eckie ✕ Leckie
Scotland's leading educational publishers

D0316860

SNAP REVISION

POETRY BY CAROL ANN DUFFY

For National 5 and Higher English

REVISE FOR YOUR SQA EXAMS

David Cockburn

SNAP REVISION POETRY BY CAROL ANN DUFFY

Published by Collins
An imprint of HarperCollinsPublishers
1 London Bridge Street,
London, SE1 9GF

© HarperCollinsPublishers Limited 2018

9780008306687

First published 2018

10 9 8 7 6 5 4 3 2 1

All rights reserved. No part of this publication may be reproduced, stored in a retrieval system, or transmitted in any form or by any means, electronic, mechanical, photocopying, recording or otherwise, without the prior written permission of the Publisher or a licence permitting restricted copying in the United Kingdom issued by the Copyright Licensing Agency Ltd., 90 Tottenham Court Road, London W1T 4LP.

British Library Cataloguing in Publication Data.

A CIP record of this book is available from the British Library.

Printed in United Kingdom.

Commissioning editor: Gillian Bowman
Managing editor: Craig Balfour
Author: David Cockburn
Proofreader: Jess White
Project manager and editor: Project One Publishing Solutions, Scotland
Typesetting: Jouve
Cover designers: Kneath Associates and Sarah Duxbury
Production: Natalia Rebow

ACKNOWLEDGEMENTS

The author and publisher are grateful to the copyright holders for permission to use quoted materials.

Collected Poems by Carol Ann Duffy. Published by Picador, 2015. Copyright © Carol Ann Duffy. Reproduced by permission of the author c/o Rogers, Coleridge & White Ltd., 20 Powis Mews, London W11 1JN

From the author:
I am most grateful to Peter Doughty, ex-Principal Examiner, OCR A-level English literature, for his knowledge and inspiring understanding of Duffy's poetry. I am also indebted to Leckie and Leckie's highly talented team, whose support and consideration goes beyond expectation. And I should like to thank Kevin Cockburn without whose endless encouragement and patience this book would never have been written.

Every effort has been made to trace copyright holders and obtain their permission for the use of copyright material. The author and publisher will gladly receive information enabling them to rectify any error or omission in subsequent editions. All facts are correct at time of going to press.

Contents

This book will help you revise everything you need to know about the poetry of Carol Ann Duffy and the exam. You can either read it through or turn to the sections relevant to you when you revise.

This book will help you with all the stages of revision. It provides:

- a detailed analysis of all six poems; see pages 6–33

- an examination of Duffy's themes and/or ways in which character is presented; see pages 34–41

- an analysis of Duffy's techniques by which those themes and/or character presentation have been portrayed/conveyed; see pages 42–53

- help with exam preparation, including exam-style questions with comments and possible answers showing how marks would be allocated; see pages 54–71

- mock exam questions to provide practice; see pages 72–73

- a glossary of useful terms – handy for a quick revision check; see pages 74–75

- possible answers to all questions; see pages 76–80.

This is book is aimed at students taking National 5 and at those taking Higher. All of the material is relevant to both courses except course-specific details that are denoted either N5 or H. Use these icons to guide you to the sections appropriate to your course.

Introduction

Approach to Carol Ann Duffy's poetry

Duffy's life

Carol Ann Duffy was born in Glasgow in 1955 and moved with her parents and brothers to Stafford in England when she was just six years old. She is currently Professor of Contemporary Poetry at Manchester Metropolitan University. She is the UK's first woman, the first Scot, and the first LGBT (lesbian, gay, bisexual and transgender) person to hold the position of Poet Laureate. If you want to read more of her poetry, she has had many anthologies published.

The Poet Laureate is expected to write verse for significant national occasions. Duffy has held the post since 2009, having been appointed by the Queen on the advice of the then Prime Minister. The role dates back to 1616.

Duffy's poetry

All of Duffy's poems deal with aspects of human existence, mainly relationships, women, emotions, the inequalities within society – concerns that we all share. Sometimes she presents characters in her poems: for example, she presents the character of Mrs Midas (pages 6 and 10), the character in *Valentine* (page 14), and the character of the *War Photographer* (page 30), although his character is described by a third person, unlike the other five poems you are studying, which are in the first person.

Mrs Midas and *Valentine* are known as **dramatic monologues**, a form of poetry much used by Duffy. A dramatic monologue is where:

- the poem is in the **first person**
- a **persona**/speaker is addressing someone unknown (not necessarily the reader)
- the speaker unwittingly and/or deliberately reveals aspects of their character
- the reader becomes increasingly aware of the gap between what the speaker says and underlying aspects of their character.

Although *Originally*, *In Mrs Tilscher's Class* and *The Way My Mother Speaks* are also in the first person, they aren't really dramatic monologues, simply because the speaker appears less crafted. Nevertheless, these poems are about more than Carol Ann Duffy's personal experiences – they are about identity and transformation, about how the present emerges from the past. In other words, as with all her poetry, she explores themes.

Themes

The theme of a poem is what you think the poem is about: relationships, love, unrequited love, isolation, rejection, loneliness, joy, greed, death, discovery, revenge, doubt, regret, hypocrisy – the list is endless.

It is important to realise that a poem is, of course, about itself, the particular theme or narrative that it expresses, but equally the theme or narrative or character presentation has also a universal significance. The poem ultimately is making a comment on human nature, reflecting on our human condition – true in itself but also universally true.

In *Originally*, for example, Carol Ann Duffy writes about moving not just house but countries. The poem gives details about the actual journey to the new home and details of her reaction when she started living there. But though the poem is about a particular move in a particular young girl's life, it also resonates with everyone who has moved to a new house, especially from one city to another or one country to another. The poem also examines identity – all those influences by our peer group, geography and culture that make each one of us who we are.

Textual analysis

In your approach to the Duffy poems, it is important that you keep in mind that the Scottish Text question is an exercise in textual analysis. At both N5 and Higher, in your response to the questions, you need to be able to refer to relevant parts of the text and then analyse your reference appropriately.

Textual analysis differs from RUAE (Reading for Understanding, Analysis and Evaluation, that is, close reading) in that it almost always involves the analysis of the writer's technique, though, of course, the RUAE paper can also ask about technique.

With all six of Carol Ann Duffy's poems, you need to know:

- the themes and issues explored or conveyed by each of the poems you are studying
- the various language techniques by which the themes are conveyed.

Language techniques

In N5 and in Higher, questions will invite you to refer to language techniques. As with RUAE, the term 'language' covers sentence structure, **word choice, imagery, contrast** and **tone**. But you are studying poetry, therefore you must know about structural techniques such as verse structure, **rhyme** (where appropriate), **rhythm**, sentence structure, **enjambement** and contrast. You also need to be clear as to what is meant by imagery: techniques such as **metaphor** (including **simile** and **personification**), **oxymoron**, as well as **synecdoche** and **transferred epithet**; there are also sound techniques that you should know, such as **alliteration**, **assonance** and **onomatopoeia**.

Each of these terms is defined in the Glossary of useful terms on pages 74–75.

You need to have studied the poems thoroughly and know them well. You could record them on your phone so that you can listen to them as often as possible. The N5 8-mark and the Higher 10-mark questions demand that you refer to poems other than the printed one, so you must be able to quote from other poems relevant to the question.

Mrs Midas 1

It was late September. I'd just poured a glass of wine, begun
to unwind, while the vegetables cooked. The kitchen   **A**
filled with the smell of itself, relaxed, its steamy breath
gently blanching the windows. So I opened one,
5   then with my fingers wiped the other's glass like a brow.
He was standing under the pear tree snapping a twig.   **B**

Now the garden was long and the visibility poor, the way
the dark of the ground seems to drink the light of the sky,   **C**
but that twig in his hand was gold. And then he plucked
10   a pear from a branch – we grew Fondante d'Automne –   **D**
and it sat in his palm like a lightbulb. On.
I thought to myself, Is he putting fairy lights in the tree?   **E**

He came into the house. The doorknobs gleamed.
He drew the blinds. You know the mind; I thought of   **F**
15   the Field of the Cloth of Gold and of Miss Macready.
He sat in that chair like a king on a burnished throne.
The look on his face was strange, wild, vain. I said,
What in the name of God is going on? He started to laugh.   **G**

I served up the meal. For starters, corn on the cob.
20   Within seconds he was spitting out the teeth of the rich.
He toyed with his spoon, then mine, then with the knives, the forks.   **H**
He asked where was the wine. I poured with shaking hand,
a fragrant, bone-dry white from Italy, then watched   **I**
as he picked up the glass, goblet, golden chalice, drank.   **J**

25   It was then that I started to scream. He sank to his knees.
After we had both calmed down, I finished the wine   **K**
on my own, hearing him out. I made him sit
on the other side of the room and keep his hands to himself.
I locked the cat in the cellar. I moved the phone.   **L**
30   The toilet I didn't mind. I couldn't believe my ears:

how he'd had a wish. Look, we all have wishes; granted.
But who has wishes granted? Him. Do you know about gold?   **M**
It feeds no one; aurum, soft, untarnishable; slakes
no thirst. He tried to light a cigarette; I gazed, entranced,
35   as the blue flame played on its luteous stem. At least,
I said, you'll be able to give up smoking for good.   **N**

Context

According to Greek mythology, King Midas wished that everything he touched would turn to gold. The god Dionysus granted his wish, but Midas soon realised that he would quickly die of starvation. Duffy adapts and updates the story, telling it from the **perspective** of Midas' long-suffering wife, Mrs Midas.

Themes

The poem is really about the couple's relationship and the extent to which it deteriorates because of greed. It is about love, separation, loss and regret. It is also about change.

Structure

The poem is a **dramatic monologue**, a form of poetry in which a speaker or **persona** (not the poet) addresses someone unknown, and in the process he/she reveals unwittingly unpleasant aspects of character. It is in eleven 6-line verses of unequal length and irregular rhythm, echoing the chaos of the couple's crisis. Although Mrs Midas is speaking (**first-person narration**), nevertheless the poet is in the background manipulating the character – to what extent is Duffy poking fun? Our impression of Midas himself is created by Mrs Midas, who, in turn, is created by Carol Ann Duffy.

Annotations

A Lines 1–4: a relaxed atmosphere is created by 'late September', a mellow time, where Mrs Midas unwound with 'a glass of wine' while 'the vegetables cooked', creating a scene of quiet domesticity. **Word choice** – 'filled with the smell of itself' and 'relaxed' – suggest tranquillity and gratification. The **personification** and **enjambement** – 'steamy breath / gently blanching the windows' form a **contrast** with her husband's activities in the next verse.

B Line 6: in the word choice of 'snapping a twig', the **onomatopoeic** 'snapping' creates a discordant (unpleasant) **tone**.

C Lines 7–9: the first word 'Now' introduces the narrative. Word choice – 'visibility poor', 'dark of the ground', 'drink the light of the sky' – all suggest foreboding; the word 'dark' suggests sinister or ominous, though the 'twig in his hand was gold' is a reference to the Midas touch.

Annotations (continued)

D Lines 10–11: the **parenthetical** ' – we grew Fondante d'Automne – ' reveals her pretentiousness in naming an old variety of French pear. The pear is golden, and the expression 'sat in the palm of his hand like a light bulb' adds **humour**, reinforced by the **minor one-word sentence** 'On.'. The **simile** 'like a light bulb' compares the pear to a light bulb in gold colour and shape.

E Line 12: humour – the reference to fairy lights: she doesn't know what is happening; she is oblivious to the seriousness of what her husband is doing.

F Lines 13–16: three short sentences create the impression of Mrs Midas talking to the reader. 'He drew the blinds' suggests he wants privacy. The chatty tone continues – 'You' addresses the reader. Gold is a **symbol**, 'the Field of the Cloth of Gold' (reference to a meeting between Henry VIII and Francis I of France near Calais where everything was gold) and 'Miss Macready' (who claimed to be Mrs Midas' history teacher, teaching about the historic meeting); the now-golden blinds; the simile 'like a king on a burnished throne' is from Shakespeare's *Anthony and Cleopatra*. Although these references give authenticity to the poem, they also seem slightly mischievous.

G Lines 17–18: the pile-up of **adjectives** – 'strange, wild, vain' – describes his sudden realisation of his unprecedented power and wealth. However, 'vain' also reveals her criticism of her husband. In line 18, the question expresses her puzzlement, but he only laughs – revealing their contrasting reactions.

H Lines 19–21: the everyday tone – 'I served up the meal' – is an apparent attempt by Mrs Midas at normality. 'For starters' is chatty, but it is also humorous and **paronomastic**, playing on the **colloquial** phrase 'for starters' and the menu reference 'for the starter'. The humorous **metaphor** – 'spitting out the teeth of the rich' – suggests that the corn has turned to gold, has become inedible or that his teeth have splintered on the corn, revealing the beginning of the problems brought by his 'gift'; 'of the rich' is used **ironically**; 'toyed' suggests playfulness on Midas' part, that he has fun in turning everything he touches into gold.

I Lines 22–23: 'I poured with shaking hand' suggests that her anxiety is increasing, whereas 'a fragrant, bone-dry white from Italy', and the adjectives 'fragrant' and 'bone-dry' ('bone' with its underlying suggestion of death), suggest her pretentiousness – despite being nervous, she cannot resist trying to impress.

J Line 24: by contrast, the seriousness of the transformation of a simple glass into a golden chalice is highlighted by the **alliteration** of the **guttural** 'g' sound, softened slightly by the alliteration of the rich, **liquid** 'l' sound, the effect of which is to suggest dangerous luxury; 'golden chalice' references Macbeth's poisoned chalice, suggesting that the chalice out of which Midas is about to drink could kill him. By placing the word 'drank' at the end of the sentence, the line and the verse, Midas' fate is highlighted.

K Lines 25–26: the opening explains the result of 'drank' – it caused her to scream, he sank to his knees – all very **dramatic**; but first, she 'finished the wine', suggesting nervousness or self-centredness.

L Lines 27–30: the series of short phrases reveals her control over the extraordinary situation with its moments of humorous ordinariness: he is made to sit elsewhere, 'keep his hands to himself', and, though she feared what might happen to the cat and the phone, nevertheless the humour of 'The toilet I didn't mind' again suggests her love of ostentation.

M Lines 30–34: the enjambement between verses 5 and 6 contributes to the drama of the story – we want to know what she couldn't believe. The use of **antanaclasis** – 'granted' and 'granted' – creates a pun, and the **rhetorical question** implies that, except for 'Him', highlighted by the **monosyllabic**, one-word, minor sentence, dreams are naïve. In lines 33 and 34, she **lists** the valuelessness of gold; the word choice of the Latin 'aurum' (gold) again exposes her affectation while 'untarnishable' is neutral in tone.

N Lines 34–36: her criticism of gold ends abruptly with her contrasting joke about his being 'able to give up smoking for good'.

> ## Question
>
> Look at lines 19–24.
>
> By referring to two examples of language, explain how Duffy makes it clear that something dramatic is happening.   4

Separate beds. In fact, I put a chair against my door,   **O**
near petrified. He was below, turning the spare room
into the tomb of Tutankhamun. You see, we were passionate then,
40 in those halcyon days; unwrapping each other, rapidly,
like presents, fast food. But now I feared his honeyed embrace,   **P**
the kiss that would turn my lips to a work of art.

And who, when it comes to the crunch, can live   **Q**
with a heart of gold? That night, I dreamt I bore
45 his child, its perfect ore limbs, its little tongue
like a precious latch, its amber eyes   **R**
holding their pupils like flies. My dream-milk
burned in my breasts. I woke to the streaming sun.

So he had to move out. We'd a caravan
50 in the wilds, in a glade of its own. I drove him up
under cover of dark. He sat in the back.   **S**
And then I came home, the woman who married the fool
who wished for gold. At first I visited, odd times,
parking the car a good way off, then walking.

55 You knew you were getting close. Golden trout
on the grass. One day, a hare hung from a larch,   **T**
a beautiful lemon mistake. And then his footprints,
glistening next to the river's path. He was thin,
delirious; hearing, he said, the music of Pan   **U**
60 from the woods. Listen. That was the last straw.

What gets me now is not the idiocy or greed
but lack of thought for me. Pure selfishness. I sold   **V**
the contents of the house and came down here.
I think of him in certain lights, dawn, late afternoon,   **W**
65 and once a bowl of apples stopped me dead. I miss most,
even now, his hands, his warm hands on my skin, his touch.   **X**

Annotations

O Lines 37–39: the **minor sentence** at the beginning of verse 7 highlights the change in their relationship – they have now separated. The pun on 'petrified' continues the humorous **tone** – 'petrified' literally means 'turned to stone' and Mrs Midas is petrified (afraid) that she is going to be petrified (turned into gold). The **enjambement** in lines 38–39 emphasises 'into the tomb of Tutankhamun', reinforced by the **internal rhymes** 'room', 'tomb' and 'Tutankhamun'; moreover, the **assonance** of the long 'oo' sounds adds a humorous touch.

P Lines 37–42: their separation is further emphasised by the **contrast** between 'Separate beds', 'He was below' (on a different floor) – they are now physically separate – with 'we were passionate then' – when they were previously emotionally, sexually together. 'You see' continues the use of chatty informality. The **image** 'halcyon days' signposts a perfect time in the past; 'unwrapping each other' suggests their close sexual relationship; and though the **simile** 'like presents, fast food' suggests the joy in their relationship, 'presents' and 'fast food' are by nature transient (consumed quickly), like their relationship; 'fast food' has the **connotations** of being instant and not very satisfying. The **conjunction** 'But' introduces a change in direction – now she fears his 'honeyed embrace', where the **double entendre** combines the sexual connotations of 'honeyed' along with its now deadly connotations, developed by the last line making clear that his sexual advances could make her beautiful ('a work of art') but no longer human.

Q Lines 43–44: the conjunction 'And' not only begins a new sentence but also the new verse – isolating and highlighting the **irony**: the expression 'heart of gold' is usually complimentary, but here Mrs Midas subverts it, referring to his heart made of gold, implying the difficulties of living with perfection.

R Lines 44–48: the dream indicates that she wants a child, representing innocence, the idea quickly contrasted by disturbing images – 'its little tongue / like a precious latch', where the enjambement highlights the simile suggesting the child's tongue is hard and latched onto Mrs Midas; the 'amber eyes' (golden colour) 'holding their pupils like flies', fossilised in the viscous resin suggests death in life; she cannot have a normal child because of Midas' 'gift'. The compound noun 'dream-milk' conveys her longing for a child, while the **alliteration** of the **plosive** in 'burned in my breasts' emphasises her frustration; the entire dread is a **synecdochic** representation of her frustration at what his 'gift' has ironically denied her. The **personification** of the 'streaming sun' is a reminder that she is constantly surrounded by gold.

Annotations (continued)

S Lines 49–54: the **declarative sentence** 'So he had to move out' marks the finality of their relationship. Their earlier togetherness, shown by 'We'd a caravan / in the wilds', is contrasted with her determination to have him isolated – 'I drove him' (she is in control), 'under cover of dark' (he is hidden because she is embarrassed) and 'He sat in the back' are all a measure of how separated they have become. 'And then I came home' – the 'And' isolating and highlighting her determination to be apart. The alliteration of the 'w', the **assonance** of the 'oo' sound and her use of **third person** in 'the woman who married the fool / who wished for gold' all add to the acrimonious tone. 'At first' suggests that her visits tailed off and 'parking the car a good way off' shows her determination to remain distant.

T Lines 55–58: a series of images portrays the consequences of his wishes: 'Golden trout' – a synecdoche for inedible food; the hare 'a beautiful lemon mistake' – the **oxymoron** ('beautiful' and 'mistake') revealing how beauty can be deceptive and useless; his 'glistening' (gold) footprints by the river could suggest he is trying to get close to nature, trying to feed or wash himself.

U Lines 58–60: the **list** of adjectives – 'thin', 'delirious' – reveals his deterioration as a result of his 'gift'. It is ironic that he hears 'the music of Pan' (the Greek god of shepherds, music and nature) as it was also a Greek god who gave him the unlimited wealth which has reduced him to delusion. 'Listen. That was the last straw' – suggests she cannot cope with his instability.

V Lines 61–62: Mrs Midas reveals her self-centredness: 'but lack of thought for me' and the minor sentence 'Pure selfishness' show she thinks only of her own misery and not about what has happened to him. She 'came down here' – she has now moved further away from him.

W Lines 64–65: the tone changes: 'lights', 'dawn' (time of day), 'late afternoon' and the fruit – 'bowl of apples' (Golden Delicious) – all take the reader back to the opening of the poem; 'stopped me dead' suggests she suddenly realises what might have been.

X Line 66: the rhythm of the last line is slow, each item on the list expanding on the one before – though the irony highlighted by the repetition of 'hands' is further emphasised by 'touch' – 'his touch', after all, was the cause of the problem.

Question

N5 Look at lines 49–54.

By referring to two examples of language, explain how the character of Mrs Midas is presented. 4

H Look at lines 49–54.

By referring to two examples of language, analyse how the character of Mrs Midas is presented. 4

Valentine

Not a red rose or a satin heart. **A**

I give you an onion. **B**
It is a moon wrapped in brown paper.
It promises light
5   like the careful undressing of love. **C**

Here. **D**
It will blind you with tears
like a lover. **E**
It will make your reflection
10   a wobbling photo of grief. **F**

I am trying to be truthful. **G**

Not a cute card or a kissogram. **H**

I give you an onion.
Its fierce kiss will stay on your lips, **I**
15   possessive and faithful
as we are,
for as long as we are.

Take it. **J**
Its platinum loops shrink to a wedding ring, **K**
20   if you like.
Lethal. **L**
Its scent will cling to your fingers, **M**
cling to your knife.

Context

St Valentine, a 3rd century Roman priest, has been regarded as the patron saint of love since the 11th century and is commemorated on 14 February, when lovers exchange cards and presents. Duffy is suggesting the gift of an onion is more realistic than giving clichéd, commercialised gaudy tat (cheap, shiny items of poor quality).

Themes

In this poem, Duffy is exploring the nature of love and relationships while challenging conventional ideas of both. The main theme is stated in the middle line – 'I am trying to be honest'. She is suggesting that the notion of romantic, everlasting love and marriage is not only misguided but fallacious (deceptive): love can be short-lived and dangerous. The poem can be considered realistic or cynical or both.

Structure

The poem is a **dramatic monologue**, where the speaker addresses 'you' – his or her lover. (The gender is not specified; for the sake of simplicity, these annotations assume the persona is female.) It is in seven verses, three of which are one-line, one-sentence verses. The **free verse** structure gives the poem a direct feel, the **persona** focusing tersely on what she wants to say to her lover. The key to understanding the structural points made is to interpret 'it' and 'its' not only as the onion but as the nature of love. The poem is a developed **metaphor**, where, throughout, the onion is being compared to love. The poem also contrasts ideas of conventional love and the person's idea of truth and honesty.

Annotations

A Line 1: the 'Not', especially at the very beginning of the line, makes clear what gifts the persona is *not* going to give on Valentine's Day: the traditionally sentimental (tacky) Valentine's gifts of roses and hearts; a 'red rose' is the traditional **symbol** of love, which the persona is rejecting; similarly she rejects a gift of a 'satin heart', where 'heart' is symbolically associated with love, but here is presented as heart-shaped and glossy, shiny and therefore ostentatious and vulgar.

Annotations (continued)

B Lines 2–3: the word 'onion' suggests not only ordinariness – a common vegetable – but almost the **antithesis** of a Valentine's gift – it is mundane and cheap and very unconventional; 'moon' is a **symbol** suggesting love and romance, but here the **word choice** 'a' in front of 'moon' highlights the symbolic significance of the moon – its romantic **connotations** as well as the colour and shape of an onion; the word choice 'wrapped in brown paper' signifies the brown skin of the onion as well as the use of ordinary, cheap, everyday wrapping paper, implying that Valentine's Day wrapping paper is gaudy and **kitsch**.

C Lines 4–5: the word 'It' refers to both the onion and to love: both promise light, but both (the moon and love) only *promise* light, that is, fulfilment isn't guaranteed – love won't always illuminate, and the **enjambement** 'like the careful undressing of love' also suggests that the emotional/sexual image of undressing (getting to know each other's characters) isn't always a promise fulfilled either. The word 'love' is accentuated because it is unexpected after 'careful undressing' – by being placed at the end of the line and the verse.

D Line 6: the single-word, single-line **minor sentence** 'Here', accentuated by the **monosyllable**, suggests a domineering way of giving a present, with maybe a touch of contempt.

E Lines 7–8: an onion can 'blind you with tears', and the enjambement 'like a lover' makes clear the ambiguity of 'It': both an onion and a lover can cause tears; also, Eros and Cupid, the Greek and Roman gods of love, respectively, are depicted as blind.

F Lines 9–10: tears can distort 'your reflection', presumably in the mirror; the lover can appear as a 'wobbling photo of grief'; the word choice 'wobbling' indicates the ability of love to disorientate and unbalance, while the word 'grief' makes clear the loss and anguish that love can cause – people who give themselves to romantic love are vulnerable.

G Line 11: the single-sentence, single-line 'I am trying to be truthful' conveys the central theme of the poem – honesty is preferable to deceit. However, the fact that she is 'trying' suggests that either it is not easy to be truthful or that the lover doesn't want to hear the truth.

H Line 12: the single-sentence, single-line 'Not a cute card or a kissogram' repeats the idea in the first line of the poem, rejecting other **hackneyed** Valentine gifts. The **alliteration** of the hard 'c', the 'k' and hard 'g' **guttural** sounds draws attention to meaning, that is, to the gifts she doesn't give; the word 'cute' here has a **pejorative tone**, conveying the persona's dismissiveness of cliché.

I Lines 13–17: line 13 repeats the gift of an onion, a kind of **refrain**; 'its fierce kiss' is a **transferred epithet** – the kisser is kissing fiercely, but because the 'Its' can refer to both the onion and love, the image is quite complex: the onion's 'fierce kiss' suggests the taste of an onion is also like a kiss. In lines 14–17, there are a number of poetic devices. There is **personification** of the 'fierce kiss' staying 'on your lips, / possessive and faithful': the personification draws attention to the **contrast** of 'possessive' (unpleasant characteristic) with 'faithful' (pleasant), while enjambement causes surprise at both run-on lines – 'as we are' and 'for as long as we are', especially the latter. There is also the repetition of 'as we are', which develops the idea that even this couple cannot be guaranteed – or guarantee each other – everlasting love, a further comment by the persona on the nature of love.

J Line 18: the **imperative** (a command) 'Take it' can, of course, refer to the onion and/or love; the persona has built up her reasons for giving an onion as a present; now, in a two-word sentence in a line by itself, she instructs her lover to 'Take it' in an insistent, almost dominant tone.

K Line 19: 'platinum loops' is an example of **synecdoche**, where the image represents both the colour ('platinum') and the layers ('loops') of an onion. 'Platinum' suggests a precious, expensive metal and 'wedding ring' represents the relationship/marriage of the two lovers, but the word 'shrink', used here metaphorically, is pejorative, suggesting that the top value of platinum is diminished by being reduced to the size of a wedding ring. The image is **reductive**, demeaning even, capturing the constrained nature, both physically and emotionally, of marriage – the initial platinum loops of love (suggesting value and preciousness) are eventually reduced to a mere wedding ring, with the word 'loops' suggesting ongoing, inescapable repetitiveness.

L Line 21: although the word 'Lethal' is associated with killing, it can also mean extremely harmful. The position and shortness of the line and sentence draws attention to the violence that love can cause.

M Lines 22–23: the **repetition** of 'cling' reinforces the idea of 'scent': the scent of love and/or the onion will cling to you or to 'your knife'; the repetition of 'cling' also suggests emotional dependence, a metaphor conveying lack of escape and being smothered; the last word of the poem is 'knife', again underlining the violence of love and its ability to cut or be cutting.

> ## Question
>
> Read lines 13–17.
>
> With reference to language, explain how the persona makes clear that love is not guaranteed.   2

In Mrs Tilscher's Class

You could travel up the Blue Nile   **A**
with your finger, tracing the route
while Mrs Tilscher chanted the scenery.
"Tana. Ethiopia. Khartoum. Aswan."   **B**
5   That for an hour, then a skittle of milk   **C**
and the chalky Pyramids rubbed into dust.
A window opened with a long pole.
The laugh of a bell swung by a running child.   **D**

This was better than home. Enthralling books.   **E**
10 The classroom glowed like a sweetshop.
Sugar paper. Coloured shapes. Brady and Hindley   **F**
faded, like the faint, uneasy smudge of a mistake.
Mrs Tilscher loved you. Some mornings, you found
she'd left a gold star by your name.   **G**
15 The scent of a pencil slowly, carefully, shaved.
A xylophone's nonsense heard from another form.   **H**

Over the Easter term the inky tadpoles changed
from commas into exclamation marks. Three frogs   **I**
hopped in the playground, freed by a dunce
20 followed by a line of kids, jumping and croaking
away from the lunch queue. A rough boy   **J**
told you how you were born. You kicked him, but stared
at your parents, appalled, when you got back home.

That feverish July, the air tasted of electricity.   **K**
25 A tangible alarm made you always untidy, hot,
fractious under the heavy, sexy sky. You asked her
how you were born and Mrs Tilscher smiled   **L**
then turned away. Reports were handed out.
You ran through the gates, impatient to be grown,   **M**
30 the sky split open into a thunderstorm.

Context

In 1967, her last year of primary school, Carol Ann Duffy was taught by Mrs Tilscher. The poem deals with the child's experiences from the beginning of the school year, through to Easter and finally to the end of the year in July. The poem, then, is **autobiographical** to an extent, but it also has strong universal appeal because it deals with the maturing process at the age of 12, an experience we have all gone through.

Themes

The poem deals with that point at the end of primary school when developing adolescence promises excitement and adventure – one of the transitions of childhood. The poem, then, deals with innocence, change, growing up and anticipation of greater things to come.

Structure

The poem is **first-person narration** – the voice of the child in her final year of primary school. It is in four verses: two 8-line and two 7-line. It is written in **free verse**, with no **rhyme scheme** and no regular **rhythm**. The poem is highly rich in sensory **imagery**: sight, hearing, touch, smell, taste.

Annotations

A The title of the poem leads straight into the first line of the poem – we read on as though the title and the first three lines are all one sentence; the effect, along with the **word choice** 'You' (note the capital 'Y'), refers to the corporate response of the class, but the 'You' also instantly involves the reader.

B Line 4: the **minor one-word sentences** 'Tana. Ethiopia. Khartoum. Aswan' evoke the route of the Blue Nile, but the fact that she chants places through which the Nile flows also evokes the teaching style of the period.

C Lines 5–6: 'skittle' (as in 10-pin bowling) is a **metaphor** for the small bottle of milk given at break time. After break, the 'chalky Pyramids' have been rubbed off the blackboard, and the word choice 'chalky' and 'rubbed into dust' are **literal** – teachers used chalk and dusters to clean off the chalk – but there is also the metaphorical image of the 'dust' associated with desert conditions, and the ease with which the past can be brushed away.

Annotations (continued)

D Lines 7–8: these lines present two different images: the window is 'opened with a long pole', again evoking 1960s classrooms, with their long, high windows, but also capturing the movement and rhythm of the morning – from geography lesson for an hour, then break, the heat building up, until the **personification** – 'The laugh of a bell' – signals lunchtime; the verse conveys how happy and joyful it all was.

E Lines 9–11: the second verse begins with a **declarative sentence**, affirming her love of Mrs Tilscher's class. Then there is a series of minor sentences – 'Enthralling books', 'Sugar paper', 'Coloured shapes' – interrupted by the **simile** 'The classroom glowed like a sweetshop'. The minor sentences provide a visual snapshot conveying the excitement and appeal of the classroom while the simile suggests the classroom was as enthralling as a sweetshop; 'sugar paper', with its bright colour and rough, sometimes sparkly surface, suggests the enjoyment of craft work.

F Lines 11–13: 'Brady and Hindley', from the Manchester area, are known as the Moors Murderers, who killed young people between 1963 and 1965; people were frightened, and the use of their names, **contrasted** with the excitement of the classroom, shocks the reader. The simile – 'faded, like the faint, uneasy smudge of a mistake' – is complex: 'faded' suggests that awareness of Brady and Hindley had not disappeared, only diminished; the **alliteration** of the 'f' sound, along with the **assonance** of the long 'a' sounds ('Brady', 'faded', 'faint', 'mistake'), contrasted with the short **guttural** 'u' sound ('uneasy', 'smudge'), all add to the confusion of her feelings about the murderers; 'uneasy smudge' and 'mistake' convey the idea of an unsuccessful attempt to erase an error, but the next line 'Mrs Tilscher loved you' overtakes the memories of the murderers; the short declarative sentence brings warmth and security back to the verse.

G Lines 13–14: the **enjambement** 'you found / she'd left a gold star by your name' highlights the fact that 'Mrs Tilscher loved you', the 'gold star' evoking success.

H Lines 15–16: the 'scent of a pencil' which has been 'slowly, carefully, shaved' is not only suggestive of primary classrooms at that time, but also of the memory of pencils sharpened with a pen-knife to a fine point. The **audial** image of a 'xylophone's nonsense heard from another form' reminds readers of the sounds of a school and the **setting** in time.

I Lines 17–20: there is a change at the beginning of the third verse: the complexity of the metaphor 'inky tadpoles changed / from commas into exclamation marks' conveys not only the physical change taking place with the tadpoles, but also the metaphorical change taking place among the children. The **image** 'exclamation marks' registers, perhaps, their surprise at what is happening to their bodies, but also their increase in confidence and boldness; the image is developed by the **semantic field** (words which belong to a similar group) of 'inky', 'commas' and 'exclamation marks', all language used in the classroom. The use of 'dunce' and 'line of kids' suggests the observation is from the slightly older **persona**'s **perspective** – she is being superior and condescending; the audial image 'croaking' adds humour to the frog image.

J Lines 21–23: the **tone** becomes serious: because of the enjambement, the beginning of line 22 'told you how you were born' comes as a surprise after 'A rough boy'; now she knows about sex, heralding her loss of innocence; she is unable to deal with the knowledge and kicks him, but, later, she looks at her parents 'appalled': she has understood.

K Lines 24–26: the **transferred epithet** – 'feverish July' – along with the **synaesthesia** – 'air tasted of electricity' (electricity cannot be tasted) – convey the emerging sexual awareness of the pupils; 'feverish' suggests heat, agitation and intensity, while 'electricity' suggests excitement and being emotionally charged. In the next sentence, the word choice 'tangible alarm' conveys a concrete, physical agitation, a warning of sexual tension, the effect of which is expressed by the pile-up of adjectives – 'untidy, hot, / fractious' – all **connoting** increasing distress and confused feelings; in the transferred epithet 'heavy, sexy sky', where the epithets or **adjectives** 'heavy' and 'sexy' have been transferred, it is the speaker (and the pupils) who experience heaviness and sexual awareness.

L Lines 26–28: the use of enjambement 'You asked her / how you were born' causes 'how you were born' to come as a surprise, though 'turned away' suggests Mrs Tilscher wasn't prepared to answer the question.

M Lines 28–30: the short sentence 'Reports were handed out' suggests the conclusion of primary school, then the **kinetic** imagery – 'You ran through the gates', 'impatient to be grown', 'the sky split open', 'into a thunderstorm' – of the final conclusive sentence contrasts vividly with the gentle movements in the opening verse – 'tracing the route'. The last sentence almost explodes with energy and threat, especially with 'sky split open' and 'thunderstorm', portending the storms of adolescence to come, although there is the underlying idea of opportunities still to come.

Question

Look at lines 9–11 (from 'This was better' to 'Coloured shapes.').

By referring to two examples of language, show how the speaker makes clear her excitement in Mrs Tilscher's classroom.   4

We came from our own country in a red room
which fell through the fields, our mother singing   **A**
our father's name to the turn of the wheels.
My brothers cried, one of them bawling, *Home,*
5   *Home*, as the miles rushed back to the city,   **B**
the street, the house, the vacant rooms
where we didn't live any more. I stared
at the eyes of a blind toy, holding its paw.   **C**

All childhood is an emigration. Some are slow,
10   leaving you standing, resigned, up an avenue   **D**
where no one you know stays. Others are sudden.
Your accent wrong. Corners, which seem familiar,
leading to unimagined pebble-dashed estates, big boys
eating worms and shouting words you don't understand.   **E**
15   My parents' anxieties stirred like a loose tooth
in my head. *I want our own country*, I said.   **F**

But then you forget, or don't recall, or change,   **G**
and, seeing your brother swallow a slug, feel only
a skelf of shame. I remember my tongue
20   shedding its skin like a snake, my voice   **H**
in the classroom sounding just like the rest. Do I only think
I lost a river, culture, speech, sense of first space   **I**
and the right place? Now, *Where do you come from?*
strangers ask. *Originally?* And I hesitate.   **J**

Context

Carol Ann Duffy was aged six when she moved with her family from Glasgow to Stafford in England. The poem reflects a young person's move from one country to another.

Themes

The poem is about the ways in which the influences of geography, cultural environment, vocabulary and accent shape our personality and identity. It is also about the changes brought by growing up.

Structure

This poem is composed of three 8-line verses, related in the **first person** by a **persona** – from the point of view of a young child to begin with and then the adult looking back and reflecting on the process.

Annotations

A Lines 1–3: the **metaphor** 'red room' compares their mode of transport to a red-coloured room, very much a child's **perspective** – probably a car. The metaphor 'fell through the fields', from a child's point of view, creates the impression of going downhill, perhaps going south. Also, the internal **para-rhyme** of 'fields' and 'wheels' adds to the **rhythm** of movement; the **enjambement** 'our mother singing / our father's name' creates a surprise – we expect a song, not 'our father's name'; but sung in rhythm to the 'turn of the wheels', the song suggests a child-like chant to cheer and amuse her children.

B Lines 4–5: the **sound images** 'My brothers cried' and 'bawling' create a **contrast** with their mother's singing, highlighting the degree of their upset. Duffy uses an **italic** font to indicate and highlight the words they were bawling. In lines 5–7, the reverse direction of 'the miles rushed back to the city, / the street, the house, the vacant rooms / where we didn't live any more' has several effects: the perspective would appear to be her looking backwards – from a car's rear window; the speedily reducing reverse journey (almost like a cinematic zoom) concentrates the reader's focus on the **clause** 'where we didn't live any more', suggesting nostalgia for what they're leaving behind, further highlighted by the enjambement which places the clause at the beginning of line 7, thus emphasising their uncertainty.

Annotations (continued)

C Lines 7–8: enjambement highlights the last line of the verse, especially the **climactic** 'holding its paw', which conveys the insecurity and apprehension of a young child, seeking comfort in a beloved toy; that she 'stared' at the toy suggests her uncertainty and apprehension.

D Lines 9–12: the **declarative** first sentence of the second verse – 'All childhood is an emigration' – signals the older persona reflecting on the nature of childhood: it involves the progress from one stage to another in the process of maturing. The image is both **kinetic** – she has moved countries – and metaphorical – she is growing up, her personality, attitudes, emotions, physical appearance are changing. The use of contrast indicates the two types of change: some are 'slow', an idea reinforced by the long sentence structure, the climax – 'where no one you know stays' – is delayed by the insertion of 'leaving you standing' and 'resigned'. Then, by contrast, the short sentences – 'Others are sudden' and 'Your accent wrong' – reflect that some changes are abrupt.

E Lines 13–14: the next sentence uses **tricolon** – the list 'unimagined pebble-dashed estates', 'big boys eating …' and 'shouting words …' has the effect of drawing attention to the number and variety of 'unimagined', unpleasant scenes, building up to the climax 'shouting words you don't understand', making clear that communication is impossible.

F Lines 15–16: just as a loose tooth is annoying, partly because we can't help prodding it with our tongue, partly because we are conscious that it is always there, so the **simile** is suggesting that her ever-present awareness of her 'parents' anxieties' keeps disturbing her. The internal **rhyme** 'head' and 'said' has a concluding effect, making clear her desire to go back to Scotland. The italic font is used to signal direct speech and also for emphasis.

G Lines 17–19: although the **conjunction** 'But' at the beginning of the next verse links back to her plea for her own country, it also signals her transformation in the form of a **list:** 'you forget, or don't recall, or change'; her brother 'swallows a slug', thereby indicating the change in him, adjusting to being like the 'big boys' in the previous verse. The metaphor – '[she feels] only a skelf of shame' – suggests that she no longer feels such disgrace or embarrassment at the change in him. ('Skelf' is a Scots word meaning a small splinter that gets under the skin.)

H Lines 19–20: the simile 'my tongue / shedding its skin like a snake' compares her loss of accent to a snake losing its skin *as it grows*; the **word choice** 'snake' has undertones of deception – she is betraying her previous identity by accepting her new identity and becoming like the rest.

I Lines 21–23: the question is in the form of a list, asking what it is she has lost – aspects that gave her identity and a sense of self – but since the list is in the form of an unanswered question, she remains uncertain.

J Lines 23–24: the first question (again in italic font) is from someone who doesn't know her, but her response in the last line shows her questioning her own sense of identity, further reinforcing her uncertainty.

Question

Look at the first verse (lines 1–8).

With reference to two examples of the writer's language, show how Duffy presents the idea that the children are very young.   4

The Way My Mother Speaks

I say her phrases to myself
in my head   **A**
or under the shallows of my breath,   **B**
restful shapes moving.
5   *The day and ever. The day and ever.*   **C**

The train this slow evening
goes down England   **D**
browsing for the right sky,
too blue swapped for a cool grey.
10   For miles I have been saying
What like is it   **E**
the way I say things when I think.
Nothing is silent. Nothing is not silent.   **F**
What like is it.

15   Only tonight
I am happy and sad   **G**
like a child
who stood at the end of summer
and dipped a net   **H**
20   in a green, erotic pond. *The day*   **I**
and ever. The day and ever.
I am homesick, free, in love   **J**
with the way my mother speaks.

Context

As the **persona** travels on a train journey away from home, she reflects, revealing the closeness of the mother–daughter relationship, on the way her mother spoke and, more generally, on the nature of change.

Themes

The poem deals with many themes, particularly change and emigration from one stage to another. The entire poem can be read as a train journey, a **metaphor** to suggest the journey into adulthood. The changing scenery captures the changes experienced by the persona as she leaves the warmth and security of home for the 'cool grey' of the future. There are inevitable comparisons with *Originally*, and the explosion into adolescence suggested at the end of *In Mrs Tilscher's Class*. These poems resonate with all of us.

Structure

There are three verses: one 5-line verse and two 9-line verses. The poem is **first-person narration**, the persona almost thinking aloud as she travels by train through England. The poem captures the rhythm of the train – if you read it aloud you'll hear the rhythm.

Annotations

A Lines 1–2: in tune with the train's rhythm, the persona repeats her mother's phrases to herself – 'in my head' – suggesting the closeness she feels to her mother.

B Lines 3–4: the phrase 'under the shallows of my breath' indicates that her breath is shallow (and therefore rapid), suggesting nervousness, conscious of not wanting to be overheard, reinforcing her feelings of isolation. The 'restful shapes moving' in line 4 is an **oxymoron**: the train is moving but the scenery is stationary or maybe the scenery is moving while she sits still – the image conveys her confusion and uncertainty.

Annotations (continued)

C Line 5: the use of **italics** conveys that the words are being spoken, and the **repetition** captures the rhythm of the moving train as she recites one of her mother's sayings.

D Lines 6–9: the **transferred epithet** – 'this slow evening' – where 'slow' refers to the train rather than the evening, emphasises the train's tedious progress. The **word choice** of 'goes down England' and 'browsing' highlights the slowness of the journey; 'too blue' suggests her sunny life at home which is being swapped for the 'cool grey', with its connotations of dullness or threat of the prospect ahead; her apprehension, suggested in the first verse, is developed here.

E Lines 10–12: again, she hears her mother's voice asking *'What like is it'*, the Scots version of 'What is it like'. (Duffy's mother was Scottish, and this sentence construction is Scots.) She has been saying this phrase 'For miles', which suggests a trance-like state as she thinks about her home and her mother.

F Lines 13–14: the position of the **contradiction** and the **double negative** 'Nothing is silent. Nothing is not silent' not only suggest that in her confused thoughts she still hears her home life, but the repetition also captures the rhythm of the train which seems to echo the rhythm of her thoughts, always with her. The repetition of *'What like is it'* is like a refrain in her head.

G Lines 15–17: the word 'only' means here 'on this one occasion', on this particular train, on this particular occasion; she is both confused and excited; she is young, embarking on a journey into adulthood, with all the associated contradictory emotions: 'I am happy and sad'; the **simile** 'like a child' captures her feelings of tentativeness.

H Lines 18–20: the metaphor 'end of summer' signals the end of those long happy days at home with her mother. 'Dipped' again conveys her coyness, wariness of venturing into 'a green, erotic pond', where 'green' connotes innocence yet also suggests growth, opportunity, fresh experiences, and 'erotic' suggests sexual desire; 'erotic pond' is another transferred epithet: it isn't the pond that is erotic, instead 'pond' is a **symbol** for the situation/city she is about to enter.

I Lines 20–21: the enjambement and the repetition of her mother's saying, *'The day / and ever. The day and ever'* again captures the rhythm of the train as well as the rhythm of her thoughts.

J Lines 22–23: the final two lines express the contradictions and confusions developed throughout the poem: 'homesick' – she misses home already; 'free' – she no longer experiences restraints and the need to conform; but the final enjambement 'in love / with the way my mother speaks' not only expresses her love for her mother, but her love for her roots and her mother's voice in her head.

Question

Look at lines 6–14.

With reference to at least one example of language, show how Duffy conveys the persona's apprehension and/or confusion. 2

War Photographer

In his dark room he is finally alone   **A**
with spools of suffering set out in ordered rows.
The only light is red and softly glows,
as though this were a church and he   **B**
5   a priest preparing to intone a Mass.
Belfast. Beirut. Phnom Penh. All flesh is grass.   **C**

He has a job to do. Solutions slop in trays   **D**
beneath his hands, which did not tremble then   **E**
though seem to now. Rural England. Home again
10 to ordinary pain which simple weather can dispel,   **F**
to fields which don't explode beneath the feet
of running children in a nightmare heat.

Something is happening. A stranger's features   **G**
faintly start to twist before his eyes,
15 a half-formed ghost. He remembers the cries   **H**
of this man's wife, how he sought approval   **I**
without words to do what someone must
and how the blood stained into foreign dust.

A hundred agonies in black and white   **J**
20 from which his editor will pick out five or six
for Sunday's supplement. The reader's eyeballs prick   **K**
with tears between the bath and pre-lunch beers.
From the aeroplane he stares impassively at where   **L**
he earns his living and they do not care.

Context

Duffy describes a war photographer's life and work in global war zones, making us aware of his thoughts and feelings; the poem compares the brutalities of war with the complacency of the readers of the colour supplements, which were a separate colour magazine, an innovative feature of Sunday newspapers throughout the 1960s and 1970s.

Themes

The poem is about the horrors and anguish of war and society's attitudes to it. Mention of Belfast (Northern Ireland, UK), Beirut (Lebanon, Middle East) and Phnom Penh (Cambodia, Asia) reveals the global extent of war in the 1970s and 1980s. Duffy explores the morality of photographing war zones – the ethical acceptability of photographing the injured and dying war victims – along with complacency of people at home.

Structure

Duffy uses **third-person narration**. The poem has four 6-line verses and an *a b b c d d* rhyme scheme, with two rhyming **couplets** in each verse, making the verses tightly controlled, supporting the poem's restrained themes. She also uses **para-rhyme** in the last verse.

Annotations

A Lines 1–2: the **semantic field** of photography is used: 'dark room', 'spools' (film for cameras came in spools), 'ordered rows' (prints pegged on to string to dry), metaphorically suggesting rows of war graves – there is **irony** in that the dead now have order out of the chaos of war; 'finally alone' suggests the photographer has peace and relief from war zones. In the **transferred epithet** 'spools of suffering' (the spools aren't suffering), the photographs reveal the suffering; the alliteration of the **sibilant** highlights the image.

B Lines 3–5: the semantic field changes to that of the church: 'church', 'priest', 'Mass', the 'only light is red', suggesting the dark room but the 'red light', representing Christ and blood, near the altar in Catholic churches – all suggesting that the dark room is like a confessional. 'Red' could also represent the blood spilled in war. The **alliteration** of the **plosive** 'p' draws attention to the **image**; the **word choice** 'priest' indicates how seriously the photographer takes his job, adding to the solemn **tone**.

Annotations (continued)

C Line 6: in **contrast** to the gravity of the religious imagery, the **minor one-word sentences** list the devastation of capital cities of war-torn countries, the violence reinforced by the alliteration of the hard plosive 'b' and 'p' sounds, drawing further attention to the horrors of war. The final four-word **monosyllabic** sentence – 'All flesh is grass' – is a Biblical reference, suggesting that everything that lives perishes; the words 'flesh' and 'grass' are **synecdochic**: 'flesh' represents the dead soldiers and 'grass' represents the killing fields.

D Line 7: 'He has a job to do' – the **declarative** short sentence with six monosyllabic words introduces a change, suggesting that although he has to photograph such atrocious scenes, nevertheless he can suppress his emotions and just get on with it.

E Lines 7–9: the use of alliteration (the repeated **sibilant**) in 'solutions slop', the **onomatopoeic** 'slop' and the **assonance** of the short 'o' in 'sol' and in 'slop' create an almost hostile, harsh sound. 'Solutions' are literal – the fluid in the tray used to develop the photographs – and also **metaphoric** – the solutions to world conflict could be the display of the photographs 'beneath his hands'. His hands didn't 'tremble then', but once home, in his dark room, they 'seem to now', making clear that he is nervous, anxious and horrified when he sees the results of his work.

F Lines 9–12: 'Rural England' – with connotations of peace and tranquillity – **contrasts** with the violence and destruction in war zones. In lines 9–10, the **enjambement** emphasises the **oxymoron** 'ordinary pain', conveying contrast: the pain felt by people in England is unremarkable, unlike the pain felt by those in war zones. The use of the negative – 'don't explode' – in line 11 highlights the safety of England and further emphasises 'the feet / of running children in a nightmare heat' – the horror of seeing children desperately running from napalm (a chemical used in warfare causing severe burns).

G Line 13: the short declarative sentence ('Something is happening') suggests the photographs are appearing or something is happening to the photographer himself – or possibly both.

H Line 15: the 'half-formed ghost' of the dead man emerges in the print, but also in the photographer's mind; the word choice 'cries' recalls the anguish felt by the dead man's wife.

I Lines 16–17: 'sought approval' reveals his moral uncertainty of photographing the dead; the alliterative 'without words' suggests that either he couldn't speak the language or maybe his emotional upset prevented him from speaking; 'to do what someone must' – his job takes precedence over moral misgivings; he feels that he must show the world about the atrocities of war.

J Lines 19–21: 'A hundred agonies' makes clear the sheer number of photographs taken of appalling suffering, which contrasts with the 'five or six' picked out by the editor for 'Sunday's supplement' – the colour magazine section, not the main news section – thereby sensationalising war; Sunday supplements were the glossy parts of the newspaper.

K Lines 21–22: the enjambement 'prick / with tears' suggests the readers' tears are tiny, while the short time between 'bath' and 'pre-lunch beers' reveals their brief discomfort before they resume their easy existence; the internal rhyme 'tears' and 'beers' adds to the depressing cynicism. The words 'six' and 'prick' form a para-rhyme and create dissonance (discord), displaying the shallowness and indifference of the editor and the readers.

L Lines 23–24: the poem's conclusion – 'at where / he earns his living' recalls 'He has a job to do' (line 7), and sums up the theme – photography and warfare. Staring 'impassively' suggests that he stares unemotionally, inured (hardened) to his job, because of uncaring reactions back home – 'they' who 'do not care' refers to complacency in England. The rhyming couplet of the final two lines is summative (an effective way of creating finality), the assonance of the long 'a' sounds slowing the pace, adding to the overall despair.

Question

Look at lines 1–6.

By referring to at least two examples of language, show how Duffy creates a serious atmosphere in the first verse.

2

Knowledge about themes is essential when it comes to dealing with the final 8- or 10-mark question at both N5 and Higher. Duffy's poems cover a variety of themes and each poem covers more than one theme, as shown by the table below.

Poem	Theme		
	Nature of love	Nature of change	Nature of relationships
Mrs Midas	Lost/nostalgic love; love of wealth	Midas changed into man of greed; change in their love for each other; consequences of his 'gift'	Unsatisfying; dislike of husband's greed; controlling; ultimately possessive/regretful
Valentine	Bitter/ conditional/ ambiguous/ unconventional love; rejecting **stereotypical** ideas of love	From conventional **clichéd**, tacky ideas about Valentine gifts to original, more honest ideas about true nature of love	Love as caring but also violent/controlling/ possessive; constraints of marriage
In Mrs Tilscher's Class	Love for a teacher/ classroom	From innocence to gaining experience	Fulfilling/rewarding/ satisfying/respectful/ loving
Originally	Concern for family	Transformation brought about by moving home/ changing accent/ attitudes; adjustment	Family/brotherly; influence of family/ place/culture
The Way My Mother Speaks	Love for mother/ home	Change in direction of life, journey to new beginnings	Loving, respectful/much influenced by mother/ importance of secure family background
War Photographer	Love for humanity expressed through revulsion at complacency	From professional photographer to his bitterness at the complacency/ indifference of people at home to agonies of war	Humanity; the war-damaged victims; public complacency

Influence of past experiences	Presentation of character/role of place (to reveal theme)	Conflict/pain
Previous loving, emotionally and physically close relationship but now separated because of husband's greed	Speaker – dramatic monologue where speaker reveals unwittingly aspects of herself; husband (seen through speaker's eyes)	Conflict between Mrs Midas' values about love/physical contact and her husband's greed; gold/money is destructive
Ideas about conventional nature of love to ideas about being more honest about nature of love – can be dangerous and ephemeral	Speaker – **dramatic monologue** where speaker reveals unwittingly aspects of herself/himself	Stereotypical ideas of love and relationships and speaker's 'honest' idea that love can be short-lived and violent
From beginning of term to the end – effects on speaker	Mrs Tilscher as kind and loving; warmth of classroom; speaker's emotional and physical development	**Contrast** of Brady and Hindley to security of classroom; conflict with 'rough boy'; internal emotional conflict
Older adult reflecting on experiences of herself as young child moving from old home to new country	Speaker; family; original place and new home	Original home/what it represented and their new life; internal conflict within speaker about past and present; problems of identity
Influence of mother on speaker as she heads away from home to new experiences	Speaker's mother; home; train journey	Security of home; apprehension about journey ahead into new experiences
Experiences of war zones and current disgust at people's complacency towards the agony of war remote from idyllic home	**Third-person narration** – description of war photographer/war zones/ England/people at home	Horrors of war and people's complacency; war zones with 'Rural England'

Time

You must be able to: discuss and analyse the theme of time in the poetry of Carol Ann Duffy.

In all her poems, to a greater or lesser extent, Duffy deals with the theme of time – either the passing of time or how the past influences the present. The past can influence and even create our identity.

In Mrs Tilscher's Class

- Duffy uses time to reflect on herself as a young girl in her last year of primary school. In the geography lesson, she was 'tracing the route' while Mrs Tilscher 'chanted the scenery' – this suggests her age at the time; 'Easter term' indicates time has passed; then 'feverish July' indicates the end of the school year.

- The past begins in innocence, with references to the 'skittle of milk' – 'milk' suggesting childhood innocence; the 'running child' swinging the school bell describes child-like behaviour.

- By the last verse, the speaker reflects on the onset of adolescence – 'feverish July' **connotes** exhilaration, and 'ran through the gates' suggests her eagerness for new experiences; 'thunderstorm' connotes tumultuous yet dangerous times ahead.

Originally

- In *Originally* the older person reflects on the younger self – how moving countries transforms the little girl into an adjusted but uncertain adult.

- The poem begins in the 'red room' of their transport south as they 'fell through the fields', a journey during which her 'brothers cried' and she 'stared / at the eyes of a blind toy', suggesting she is very young and insecure.

- The first line of the last verse indicates time passing – eventually 'you forget, or don't recall, or change' – the **polysyndeton** (repetition of the conjunction) draws attention to the changes as she matures and adjusts.

- Despite now 'sounding just like the rest' in her new school, nevertheless she remains uncertain about her new identity – in the last line, she replies, when asked where she comes from, 'I hesitate'.

Mrs Midas

Of all Duffy's poems, *Mrs Midas* perhaps most reflects on the effects of the passing of time, especially on the relationship of Mrs Midas and her husband.

- The poem begins in 'late September', suggesting a mellow time of year, with Mrs Midas' kitchen 'relaxed' while she unwinds with 'a glass of wine'; it is a picture of calm domesticity, with her husband in the garden 'snapping a twig'.

- Her first reaction to his 'gift' of turning everything to gold is one of shock – 'I started to scream' – but once she had 'calmed down' she begins to take control – she 'locked the cat in the cellar' and 'moved the phone', clearly realising early on that his gift was dangerous.

- Now in control, she moves him to a caravan they had 'in the wilds', away from people, but then she moved 'down here', away from him altogether.

- Although her narrative is in the past **tense**, in the last verse, the speaker switches to the present tense, indicating that not only has time passed but their relationship is over. Yet she uses the present tense to express her regret – her present state is the result of past events.

The Way My Mother Speaks

- Duffy uses the **metaphor** of an evening train journey for establishing the passing of time. The metaphor also suggests the journey to new experiences. She uses **rhythm** to replicate the rhythm of the train journey – '*The day and ever*' – the **repetition** of which reinforces the metaphor.

- The speaker establishes the ambiguity of train movement (and time passing) by 'restful shapes moving': is it the inside of the train that is 'restful' while passing scenery creates the impression of 'shapes moving' or is it that to her the scenery is 'restful' while the train jerks about? Either way the **oxymoron** suggests at a deeper level that she is herself 'restful' and 'moving', that is, anxious, apprehensive about what lies ahead.

> ## Question
>
> With reference to the poems, show how Duffy suggests the importance of time in each.

Conflict

You must be able to: discuss and analyse the theme of conflict in the poetry of Carol Ann Duffy.

In her poems, Duffy presents both external conflict and internal, usually emotional, conflict.

War Photographer

- Both external and internal conflict pervade this poem. There is external conflict in the war zones – 'Belfast. Beirut. Phnom Penh.'. There is also internal conflict within the war photographer himself, between his emotionally detached professionalism when taking photographs in the war zones and his apprehension – his hands 'tremble' – when at home alone developing them.

- There is conflict between the 'hundred agonies' he photographs in the war zones and the 'ordinary pain' of 'Rural England'.

- He feels conflict between the cries of the wife, whose permission he sought 'without words', and the complacency of both his editor who will pick only 'five or six' photographs and the readers who will shed a momentary tear before returning to their comfortable lives.

- There is also conflict between the job he has to do and the complacency he feels in the aeroplane, staring 'impassively at where / he earns his living' (the UK) as he returns to war zones.

In Mrs Tilscher's Class

- There is conflict suggested by the image of 'Brady and Hindley' – two notorious child killers – on the one hand and the security of the classroom which 'glowed like a sweetshop' and the fact that 'Mrs Tilscher loved you'.

- There is the conflict between the 'rough boy' who told her about sex and her shock and disbelief expressed by kicking him.

- Internal conflict is suggested as she sees her parents in a different light – staring at them 'appalled' at the thought that they have sex.

- There is the hint of a conflict with Mrs Tilscher by the speaker asking her 'how you were born', already knowing the answer.

- The final conflict, expressed in the last verse, is her internal conflict – 'impatient to be grown' and the metaphor of the 'sky', associated with upbeat happiness and summer, threatening to 'split open into a thunderstorm', suggesting upheaval and the imminent storms of teenage years.

Valentine

- There is conflict between the speaker's idea of love and relationships and conventional ideas of love as **symbolised** by the traditional **clichéd** ideas of Valentine's Day – 'a red rose or a satin heart', 'a cute card or a kissogram' – which she rejects because she is 'trying to be truthful'.

- Since the speaker is addressing her lover – 'you' – there is an implied conflict when she says that love – suggesting their love for each other – will 'blind you with tears'. The **minor single-word sentence** 'Lethal' shows bluntly that the speaker thinks love can be deadly.

- There is conflict between the conventional notion that love lasts forever and her idea that love is not guaranteed to last – love can be 'possessive and faithful / as we are, / for as long as we are'; 'possessive' suggests controlling behaviour, while 'faithful' suggests loyalty.

- Conflict is symbolised by the wedding ring – the speaker uses the word 'platinum' with its **connotations** of expense and value on the one hand, and the phrase 'shrink to a wedding ring', where 'shrink' suggests the effect of marriage is to create restriction, monogamy, preventing individuals from doing as they please.

- There is also conflict between conventional notions of romantic love and her idea that it can be emotionally painful, demanding and destructive – 'Lethal.'.

> ### Question
>
> With reference to *Mrs Midas, Originally* and *The Way My Mother Speaks* show how Duffy conveys the theme of conflict in each.

Nature of Relationships

You must be able to: discuss and analyse the theme of the nature of relationships in the poetry of Carol Ann Duffy.

Throughout all her poems, in some way or another, Duffy explores the nature of relationships: with others, with partners, with family, with work.

In Mrs Tilscher's Class

- The speaker – a child – describes her last year at primary school and in so doing reflects on the nature of her relationships with her teacher and her classroom, and the relationship she has with herself.

- The fact that the title of the poem is effectively its first line relates everything in the poem to her teacher: the lessons and her relationship with Mrs Tilscher.

- She admires, with some nostalgia, Mrs Tilscher's teaching methods – being able to trace the journey up the Blue Nile and the way 'Mrs Tilscher chanted the scenery'.

- She adored her classroom with its 'Enthralling books'; the **simile** 'glowed like a sweetshop' suggests how colourful and stimulating it seemed. Sometimes Mrs Tilscher 'left a gold star by your name', an indication of the teacher's affection for the pupil as well as the pupil's ability.

- Her relationship with the 'rough boy' was different because he told her about sex – and she reacted by kicking him; her discovery then affected her relationship with her parents.

- The final verse shows how her relationship with the school and herself changed – she couldn't wait to explore the future.

Mrs Midas

- The relationship explored in *Mrs Midas* is between Mrs Midas and her husband; she discovers that his wish for gold is destructive because everything he touches turns to gold – a **metaphor** suggesting that his interest and values were mercenary and, in her opinion, destructive, while she valued a warm loving relationship.

- Their relationship descended into chaos at first as he turned cutlery into gold as well as his 'glass', which became a 'goblet', then a 'golden chalice'; she reacted by screaming while he 'sank to his knees'.

- Her initial panic turns to teasing him about now being 'able to give up smoking for good' – she has become the controlling partner in the relationship – she has decided they should live not just in separate beds but on separate floors.

- Her dream about having a baby with him is a measure of the shock and breakdown of their relationship.

- Increasingly she takes control – driving him to their caravan 'in the wilds', suggesting her embarrassment at being seen with him.

- Finally, in the last verse, the breakdown is complete, although she expresses regret, **ironically** at the loss of his hands and touch, which caused the problem in the first instance.

The Way My Mother Speaks

- In this poem, Duffy uses the metaphor of a train journey to explore the importance of the speaker's relationship with her mother. The intimacy of the mother–daughter relationship is made clear by the speaker stating that 'I say her phrases to myself / in my head / or under shallows of my breath'.

- The **repetition** of her mother's saying – *'The day and ever. The day and ever.'* – emphasises just how much her mother means to her and how close she feels to her even though she is on a train journey away from her.

- The **assonance** of the 'oo' sound in 'too blue' draws attention to the image – the sunny, warm comfort of home, which she is swapping for 'a cool grey' sky, less pleasant, slightly threatening.

- The **paradoxical** 'Nothing is silent. Nothing is not silent' makes sense if you think of it as her thoughts about home life in her head – she can hear them (to the rhythm of the train), but at the same time she doesn't 'hear' them in that they aren't said out loud, but they are constantly with her.

- The title of the poem strongly suggests that what matters is the *way* her mother speaks, and the use of **italics** echoes the words her mother said, that is, it's the sound of her mother in her head that measures the closeness of their relationship.

> ## Question
>
> Explore the nature of relationships in *Valentine* and *War Photographer.*

Common Techniques

Poem	Sound Effects	Enjambement/ Sentence Structure	Imagery		
			Comparison/ Central Image	Representation/ Symbolism	Contrast
Mrs Midas	p45	p47, p53	p48–49	✓	p51
Valentine	✓	p46, p52–53	✓	p50	✓
In Mrs Tilscher's Class	✓	p46, p52	p48	✓	✓
Originally	✓	✓	p48	p50	✓
The Way My Mother Speaks	✓	p47, p52	✓	✓	✓
War Photographer	p45	p52	✓	✓	p51

Poetic techniques used in Duffy's poetry

The table opposite outlines the use of common techniques in all six poems, with page references to specific examples in this book (a tick (✓) indicates that a technique is used in a poem but is not discussed in detail).

The term **free verse** refers to poems that do not have regular **rhythm** or **rhyme**. The lines of such poems are structured to capture the rhythms of everyday speech, which means the rhythm follows the pauses and pulses of spoken English. The main technique in achieving this effect is **enjambement** – the important unit of sense is the sentence and not necessarily the line structure. Duffy's poetry follows the natural rhythms of speech. *War Photographer* is the exception since it has a **rhyme scheme**.

Themes are conveyed by techniques. In the Scottish Text section of the exam, most of the questions will be about language, a term which covers sentence structure, **contrast**, **imagery**, **word choice** and **tone**. Some questions ask about a specific technique, such as word choice or imagery. You need also to be aware of techniques that are associated with poetry, such as particular sound effects and enjambement, which you may want to refer to in your answers.

You need to be able to analyse the effectiveness of various images: for example, **metaphor**, **simile**, **personification**. But these aren't the only images – there is also **synecdoche**, **symbolism**, **oxymoron** and **onomatopoeia**.

These different techniques can be classified: there are three major poetic techniques (although they aren't restricted to poetry):

- devices of comparison
- devices of representation
- devices of contrast (or paradox).

You need also to know about how Duffy uses rhythm – an important technique in her poetry.

You must be able to: discuss and analyse the use of sound effects in the poetry of Carol Ann Duffy.

Vowel sounds and consonant sounds

Sound is an important aspect of both poetry and prose. By the word 'sound', we mean the sound that we make when we speak.

There are five main vowels in English – *a, e, i, o* and *u*. We can pronounce those vowels as in *hate, feed, pine, slope* and *cute.* These are known as long vowel sounds. We can also pronounce these same vowels with a short vowel sound as in *hat, fed, pin, slop* and *cut.* Long vowel sounds tend to be more pleasant than short vowel sounds.

The other letters of the alphabet are known as consonants. Consonants can be grouped, according to the type of sound they make, as shown in the table below.

Letter	Example	Type of sound	Effect of sound
b, p	bang, paper	plosive	hard, violent
hard c, hard g, qu, k	cat, goal, queen, kill	guttural	harsh, unpleasant, violent
d, t	dentist, tooth	dental	neutral, depends on vowel sound
f, th, v	face, that, verse	fricative	can be a neutral sound, depending on vowel sound – some fricatives with short vowel sounds can be harsh
l, w, y	liquid, wool, you	liquid	mellifluous and pleasant, but the *w* sound can be mean (you make the 'w' by pursing lips together, a mean shape)
m, n	murmur, number	nasal	usually pleasant but can be unpleasant when muffled (note the nasals)
soft c, s, z	cell, silence, zodiac	sibilant	soporific or hissing
r	reef	rolling	almost like a vowel

The repetition of a vowel sound is called **assonance** (for example, the 'oo' sound in 'too blue') while the repetition of a consonant is called **alliteration** (for example, 'glass, goblet').

Onomatopoeia is where the sound of a word suggests the thing it names – for example, 'bang' represents a sudden explosive noise. Duffy rarely uses onomatopoeia, but she does use very effectively the other sound devices of alliteration and assonance.

The following example of alliteration is from *War Photographer*:

> Solutions slop in trays
> Beneath his hands

where the repeated use of the sibilants (the 's' and 'sh' sounds) creates an unpleasant sound, replicating not only the noise of the liquid in the developing tray but also suggesting a hissing, disturbing sound, anticipating the horrifying image about to appear in the developing photograph.

Assonance achieves the rhyme pattern *a b b c d d* in *War Photographer*.

In *Mrs Midas*, Duffy uses assonance in the line:

> as he picked up the glass, goblet, golden chalice, drank.

There is obvious alliteration of the guttural ('g' in 'glass, goblet, golden'), but the assonance of the 'a' and 'o' sounds has the effect of linking the words, suggesting the speedy process of the transformation of glass to gold.

Question

With reference to *Valentine*, show how Duffy's use of alliteration helps draw attention to her dismissal of the bad taste encouraged by Valentine's Day.

Enjambement

You must be able to: discuss and analyse the use of enjambement in the poetry of Carol Ann Duffy.

Poetry is different from other literary genres in that poems are written in relatively short lines whereas in prose sentences can be very long. Traditionally, a line of poetry is **end-stopped**, that is, the line is complete in itself, thus creating a pause for the reader at the end of each line.

In the poetic device **enjambement**, sentence structure does not fit the line structure. In fact, sentence structure takes precedence over line structure, and lines run on from one to the next, as shown in these lines from *In Mrs Tilscher's Class*:

> Over the Easter term the inky tadpoles changed
> from commas into exclamation marks. Three frogs
> hopped in the playground, freed by a dunce
> followed by a line of kids, jumping and croaking
> away from the lunch queue.

The first line 'spills over' onto the next, the second onto the third and so on. This pattern continues for the rest of the verse.

Often, the poet puts a caesura or pause somewhere in the line in order to force the sentence to spill over onto the next line. Note that in the second line above, there is a full stop after 'marks'. This forces the new sentence beginning with 'Three frogs' to spill over onto the next line.

The study of poetry is all about the study of form, how verses are structured. Unlike prose, poetry is *deliberately* written in lines – and you must pay attention to line endings. Some poems use end-stopped lines, where there is a natural break at the end of the line. For example, Duffy uses end-stopped lines at the beginning of *Valentine*:

> Not a red rose or a satin heart.

> I give you an onion.
> It is a moon wrapped in brown paper.

We pause at the end of each line. But often, Duffy uses enjambement, where there is a deliberate line break – that is, the sentence structure is spilled over two (or more) lines. Here is an example from *Valentine*:

> It will blind you with tears
> like a lover.

In prose, this sentence would be fairly unremarkable: 'It will blind you with tears like a lover.' But this is poetry, so we naturally pause at the end of the word 'tears' (the line break), which causes the next line to come as a surprise: 'like a lover' and makes us think about the meaning of the comparison.

Look at the next example, from *The Way My Mother Speaks*:

> Only tonight
> I am happy and sad
> like a child
> who stood at the end of summer
> and dipped a net
> in a green, erotic pond.

There are five line breaks in this sentence, each one of which is highly effective in creating the surprise we feel at the following line. However, the main effect is to make us hesitate and think carefully about the implications of the line that follows the break. We become more aware of the **simile** ('like a child'), the **metaphor** ('the end of summer') and the **personification** ('a green, erotic pond').

Throughout your study of Duffy's poetry, be aware of the significance of enjambement – the importance of line breaks.

Effects of enjambement

What are the effects of enjambement?

- Because we are used to pausing at the end of a line of poetry, we hesitate a bit, which may make what comes at the beginning of the next line a surprise – sometimes we are taken aback. In the previous extract from *In Mrs Tilscher's Class*, the words 'from commas into exclamation marks' almost shock us, thus creating a **dramatic** effect by drawing attention to the nature of the change to the tadpoles and, by extension, to the children.

- Often enjambement reflects the thoughts of the person as he/she recounts the experience being presented. For example, in *Mrs Midas*, the enjambement reflects Mrs Midas' thoughts as she relates how she feels about her husband.

- Because enjambement prioritises sentence structure over line structure, the poem reads more like prose, making it more accessible to the reader.

Question

Look carefully at *The Way My Mother Speaks*.

Show how Duffy uses enjambement effectively.

Imagery: Comparison

You must be able to: discuss and analyse the use of comparison in the poetry of Carol Ann Duffy.

Devices of comparison include **metaphor, simile** and **personification**. In these techniques, one thing is compared to another, but they do so in slightly different ways. For example:

* metaphor – saying something *is* something else (the boy *was a tiger* in the fight)
* simile – saying something *is like* something else (the boy *was like a tiger* in the fight)
* personification – attributing human-like qualities to an inanimate object (*the car protested* as it was driven uphill)

Often you are asked to explain or analyse a metaphor (or simile or personification). To do so, it sometimes helps to establish the literal meaning of the term to which the comparison is made – in this case, 'a tiger'. How does a tiger fight? Work out all the **connotations**, and, if the boy fought viciously, fiercely, ferociously, then the metaphor is effective.

Metaphor is used to end *In Mrs Tilscher's Class*:

> You ran through the gates, impatient to be grown,
> the sky split open into a thunderstorm.

These lines are metaphorical – 'ran through the gates' suggests not just physical movement but also the desire to leave the child-like stage of primary school life behind, racing towards the adolescent life to come, and 'thunderstorm' is a metaphor that suggests upheaval and emotionally wild times ahead; 'sky split open' suggests the adult world opening up ahead with all its problems.

A whole poem can be metaphorical. For example, *Mrs Midas* is a very complex poem – the story is a metaphor for the danger of wishes and dreams. Midas and Mrs Midas have different dreams: his is for wealth and hers for intimacy and family life, and it is the incompatibility of these dreams that leads to their separation and ultimate unhappiness.

Similes use 'like' or 'as'. For example, in *Originally*, Duffy writes that the **persona** remembers her 'tongue / shedding its skin like a snake'. Snakes shed their skin as they grow, therefore the simile suggests that the persona is shedding her previous accent as she matures and becomes used to her new home.

In personification, an inanimate object is given the qualities of a human being. For example, in *Mrs Midas*, the persona describes the kitchen:

> The kitchen
> filled with the smell of itself, relaxed, its steamy breath
> gently blanching the windows.

In this image, the kitchen has been given human characteristics – 'filled with the smell of itself' suggests that the kitchen is alive and has been cooking, producing its own smells.

The personification is extended by 'its steamy breath / gently blanching the windows', reinforcing the living nature of the kitchen by suggesting that it can breathe steam onto the windows, thereby capturing the results and effects of the cooking.

Transferred epithet is another poetic technique of comparison. In the lines from *Mrs Midas* above, the kitchen is described as 'relaxed'. However, it is really Mrs Midas herself who is relaxed, so the epithet (description) 'relaxed' has been transferred from her to her kitchen. In a transferred epithet there is often an unexpected combination of two words that don't normally link together. For example, from *In Mrs Tilscher's Class*, the persona uses the image 'sexy sky' – it isn't the sky that is sexy, it is the children as they become aware of their bodies.

Hyperbole – the use of exaggeration for heightened effect – is another device of comparison. Duffy uses hyperbole in several poems, an example of which can be found in *Mrs Midas*:

> He was below, turning the spare room
> into the tomb of Tutankhamun.

Duffy uses hyperbole to compare the spare room to Tutankhamun's tomb, an effective way of establishing the extent to which his 'gift' was turning everything to gold. Not only was the Pharaoh's tomb lavishly decorated with gold and contained golden artefacts, but the Pharaoh's death mask was gold. The comparison suggests the amount of gold in the spare room and introduces the idea of death.

Question

Look at *Valentine*.

Show how Duffy uses metaphor as the central image in the poem.

Imagery: Representation and Contrast

You must be able to: discuss and analyse the use of representation and contrast in the poetry of Carol Ann Duffy.

Devices of representation

Synecdoche is a device of representation, in which a part of something represents the whole or something larger. An example of synecdoche is a company's logo, where a small badge or even a word represents the entire company and its values. In a film, a vulture circling overhead can represent death.

Duffy quite frequently uses synecdoche. For example, in line 19 of *Originally*, the word 'tongue' represents the speaker's accent.

In *Originally*, the opening line refers to 'a red room', which is a **metaphor** comparing their transport – car or train – to a room, but the colour red is more synecdoche, representing threat (from the children's **perspective**), even danger. The 'blind toy' is also synecdochic, representing both her age and her need for comfort.

Symbolism is also a device of representation. For example, red roses are used as a symbol for love, white roses for friendship. In *Valentine*, the **persona** refers to 'Not a red rose or a satin heart', where 'red rose' and 'satin heart' are traditional symbols of love, but in this context they are symbols of **clichéd**, commercial tackiness.

The difference between symbolism and synecdoche

Although symbols are part of our culture, they are nevertheless quite random. We know that red roses symbolise love, but what is it about a red rose that suggests love? Nothing. The image is random, but we accept it as a symbol because it has been that way for a very long time – it has been culturally established. Although symbolism is a device of representation, the relationship between the signifier (in this case, a rose) and the signified (in this case, love) is purely arbitrary.

In contrast, synecdoche isn't at all arbitrary: synecdoche is the use of a small part of an object or image to represent the larger entity. An example is 'All hands on deck', where 'hand' represents the entire sailor. In *Valentine*, 'platinum loops' is synecdochic: 'platinum' (a precious metal) represents the colour and value of a wedding ring, while 'loops' represents the shape of the ring, which in turn represents the closed cycle of marriage. On the other hand, if we interpret the 'Its' in 'Its platinum loops' as the onion, then the image is metaphorical: the platinum loops are being compared in colour and shape to the rings of the onion. The image is as rich as it is complex, suggesting the multi-layered nature of the idea.

Devices of contrast

Another important poetic device is the use of **contrast**, a technique that Duffy quite often uses. Duffy uses contrast in these lines of *War Photographer*:

> Rural England. Home again
> to ordinary pain which simple weather can dispel,
> to fields which don't explode beneath the feet
> of running children in a nightmare heat.

The contrast is obvious: 'Rural England' and 'ordinary pain' contrast with 'running children in a nightmare heat'. 'Rural England' suggests peace and tranquillity, whereas 'nightmare heat' suggests unendurable pain; 'ordinary pain' suggests something trivial and tolerable, whereas 'children running' from napalm (implied) suggests appalling brutality.

Oxymoron is a form of contrast. Technically oxymoron is the **juxtaposition** (placing side by side) of terms that are apparently contradictory. For example, 'parting is such sweet sorrow', where 'sweet' and 'sorrow' would appear to contradict each other, but parting from someone close to you is sorrowful because you will miss him/her, but it can also be sweet because the future may bring better times.

In *Mrs Midas*, the persona describes:

> a hare hung from a larch,
> a beautiful lemon mistake.

The terms 'beautiful' and 'mistake' appear to be contradictory, but the success of oxymoron is that both terms are true: here the hare is beautiful (and lemon because it has been turned into gold) but is also a mistake because it is inedible. Midas' gift is the cause of beautiful mistakes!

Question

Look at *In Mrs Tilscher's Class*.

Show how Duffy uses devices of representation or contrast to make clear the atmosphere in the classroom.

Rhythm and Sentence Structure

You must be able to: discuss and analyse the use of rhythm in the poetry of Carol Ann Duffy.

An important aspect of arrangement in poetry is the way verses are structured. Duffy does not use **rhyme** – with the exception of *War Photographer* and some internal rhyme – and does not employ regular **rhythm**; instead she uses **verse paragraphs**, where one verse leads on from the previous verse while exploring a different aspect of content. For example, *In Mrs Tilscher's Class*, the first two verses concentrate on the speaker's experiences in Mrs Tilscher's classroom, the third verse begins to note the changes that take place after Easter, and finally the concluding verse deals with her last year in the class.

Although Duffy tends not to use regular rhythm, nevertheless rhythm is an extremely important technique of her poetry. There is the rhythm of the individual line, but also the rhythm of entire sentences which use **enjambement**. Rhythm is the variation in stressed sounds as we speak. To identify Duffy's use of rhythm, try to work out where the stress comes in each word. For example, when we say the word 'coffee', we stress the first syllable – **cof**fee. Duffy exploits rhythm to replicate speech so that what is said supports the aspect of human experience that she is exploring. An important effect is that her use of rhythm makes her poetry more like prose and therefore more accessible to the reader.

In the following lines from *In Mrs Tilscher's Class,* **bold** indicates a stressed syllable:

> You could **travel up** the **Blue Nile**

and:

> The **laugh** of a **bell** swung **by** a **run**ning **child**

The pattern is close to the rhythm of everyday speech, which makes each line less like poetry. Duffy can also use rhythm to highlight her subject matter, as shown in these lines from *The Way My Mother Speaks*:

> *The **day** and **ever**. The **day** and **ever**.*

She uses **italics** to indicate these are her mother's words and the **persona** says them over and over when on the train. But if you say them aloud you'll hear the rhythm of the train. Similarly:

> *What **like** is it.*

replicates the rhythm of a moving train.

Sentence structure is important in Duffy's poetry because she uses enjambement frequently. She uses sentence structure to achieve particular effects. She uses **minor sentences**, short sentences, **lists**, **climax**. A particular example of climax is the ending of *Valentine*:

> Its scent will cling to your fingers,
> cling to your knife.

The climactic 'knife' draws attention to one of her main themes of the poem: that love can be dangerous.

Another aspect of sentence structure used frequently by Duffy is **repetition**. The repetition of 'cling' features in the lines from *Valentine* above.

The repetition of a word does not mean that there is repetiton of meaning. In the above example, the first use of 'cling' indicates a feature of the smell of onions – it does cling to your fingers. But when Duffy repeats the word, especially by positioning it as the first word in the next line, it takes on a dark tone, almost threatening and sinister, especially when the image is then associated with the word 'knife'. The word now suggests that love can be too emotionally demanding, that lovers can become too obsessive and too emotionally dependent – and that can be dangerous, if not deadly.

Look at the last (climactic) lines of *Mrs Midas*:

I miss most,
even now, his hands, his warm hands on my skin, his touch.

The repetition of 'hands' draws attention to the idea that she misses her previous intimate relationship with him. But although 'hands' is repeated, it subtly shifts in meaning, thanks to the adjective 'warm', which suggests that, as she thinks about his hands, she increasingly remembers the tenderness and affection of their physical contact. But the **irony** in the use of 'warm hands', though it may escape Mrs Midas, doesn't escape the reader: it was these hands – 'his touch' – that caused the problem in the first place. The expression 'his warm hands', then, may suggest Mrs Midas expressing nostalgic regret, but for the reader it is a reminder of his greed, his 'Midas touch', the reason for their separation.

If you are going to discuss repetiton, then be sure to show how – in what ways – the repetiton shifts and develops meaning.

And, finally, always pay attention to Duffy's use of **tense**, another feature of sentence structure. Think about the effect of the ways in which tense is used.

- In *Valentine*, Duffy mostly uses present tense, but the ending changes to future tense, suggesting what could go wrong with their relationship.
- In *Mrs Midas*, the narrative is told in the past tense, but the ending is in the present.
- *The Way My Mother Speaks* and *War Photographer* are both in the present tense.
- *Originally* is mainly in the past tense, until in the last verse the speaker's reflections are in the present tense.
- *In Mrs Tilscher's Class* is in the past tense.

Question

Look at *In Mrs Tilscher's Class*.

Show how Duffy uses sentence structure to present the interior of Mrs Tilscher's classroom.

Preparing for the Exam

Quick tips

The Critical Reading paper consists of two sections.

Section (marks)	Assessment
Section 1 (20)	Questions assess understanding, analysis and evaluation of previously studied Scottish texts from the specified list, covering the genres of drama, prose and poetry. There will be poems and extracts from each writer.
Section 2 (20)	Critical essay questions assess understanding, analysis and evaluation of previously studied texts from drama, prose, poetry, film and television or language. **Candidates will select ONE question from a genre different from the one chosen in Section 1.**

If you are studying two Scottish texts – one text (drama or prose) or a set of poems for section 1 – then you **must** choose a **different genre** to write about in the critical essay in section 2.

If you have decided to write about the poems of Carol Ann Duffy in the Critical Essay section, then make sure that you read more widely than the six poems specified for the Scottish Text section: for example, read *Shooting Stars*, *Stealing*, *The Devil's Wife*, *The Good Teachers* (compares interestingly with *In Mrs Tilscher's Class*).

In the Critical Reading exam, for section 1 you will be given a printed poem by Carol Ann Duffy and a set of questions totalling 20 marks.

For section 2 you will be given a series of general questions (on drama, prose, poetry, film and television drama, and language). You will choose one question and use your chosen text to write an essay that answers the question. Again, the question is worth 20 marks.

Make sure that you understand what the question is asking. Most questions in section 1 will ask about language; 'language' includes sentence structure, word choice, imagery, contrast and tone as well as structural techniques, such as verse structure, rhyme (where appropriate), rhythm, sentence structure, enjambement and contrast. 'Language' also includes the sounds of the words, that is, the use of alliteration, assonance and onomatopoeia.

You should spend about 45 minutes on each section.

When writing answers to questions in section 1, there is no need to write in paragraphs – it is better to use bullet points. Make your answers as precise and analytical as you can.

Do keep checking back to the question. N5 and Higher exams are tests of reading skills – make sure you read the question carefully and accurately.

If your answer is vague, the chances are you're missing the point. Be as concise as you can.

There are three important differences between N5 questions and Higher questions.

- In N5, there is credit for all quotations/references but not in Higher.
- N5 questions use the word 'explain', for example: 'By referring to two examples of language, explain how the writer …'. However, in Higher, although the formula is similar, the word 'analyse' is often (but not always) used, for example: 'By referring to at least two examples, analyse how …'. Sometimes the Higher question is framed like this: 'Analyse how the poet's language creates a change in mood'.
- In N5 the final question is worth 8 marks whereas at Higher the final question is worth 10 marks.

In the Higher question formula, it is worth heeding the advice to use at least two examples. Since there are no marks for quotation/reference, you have to give a 'detailed/insightful comment plus quotation/reference' in order to gain 2 marks. For a more basic comment plus quotation/reference you gain 1 mark. There are 0 marks for quotation/reference alone. Therefore, for a question worth 4 marks, it is probably wiser to give three or four examples, rather than only two.

Know the poems

Preparation for the Scottish Text section is of utmost importance. It isn't enough to look at other people's annotations of poems, you really need to have a blank copy of each poem and make your own notes – the act of writing helps commit points to memory.

Also, you need to be very familiar with each poem – record the poems on your smartphone or tablet and listen to them at every opportunity; the act of listening helps commit the poems to memory, which will make it easier and quicker to support your comments with relevant quotes, especially when you have to refer to unseen poems in the 8- and 10-mark questions.

The questions

In answering the shorter questions (that is, other than the 8- and 10-mark questions), you need to be able to refer to the relevant section of the poem and then give a relevant close analytical comment.

Read the questions carefully. Both N5 and Higher papers are tests of reading skills, therefore if you make a mistake in reading a question, you will lose marks. It is useful to underline the parts of the text that you are going to quote and analyse in your answers.

Questions will be worth either 2 marks or 4 marks.

N5
- For a 2-mark question you must make one textual reference and a comment.
- For a 4-mark question you must make two textual references, each with a comment.

H
- For a 2-mark question you must make a textual reference and more detailed comments since references score 0 marks.
- For a 4-mark question you could make four textual references with four comments OR two textual references each with two detailed comments.

8- and 10-mark questions

Exam questions are designed to test your understanding of the themes and techniques of Duffy's poetry and to test if you can show understanding of more than one poem.

The question will refer you to the given poem and ask you to make reference to **at least** one other poem. For the 8- and 10-mark questions, follow this procedure:

- 2 marks are given for identifying the 'commonality' between the given poem and your chosen poem(s) as identified in the question. The question could be about theme, characterisation, a central relationship, setting, place, symbolism, imagery, personal experience, narrative technique, rhyme and/or rhythm or any other important element of poetry.

  o Identify the feature as expressed in the question (from the list above), then relate that feature to another poem or poems by the same poet.

  o You in effect are stating what you see in common between the given poem and the other poem(s) chosen by you. Mention the second poem (or the third or more).

  o If the question is about theme, it can be useful to refer to the universal aspect of the theme, as it relates to the human condition.

- 2 marks are given for reference to the given extract, commenting on whatever has been identified in the question (whether theme, characterisation, setting, symbolism, etc.). In other words, you must deal with theme and/or a technique as listed above.

  N5   o   In N5, there is 1 mark for the reference and 1 mark for the comment.

  H   o   In Higher, there are no marks for the reference, only for the comment(s).

  Make sure that the references you make can be supported by your knowledge of similar points in your chosen poem(s). Make sure that you refer to the text to support every point that you make.

- Both the N5 and Higher ask very similar questions at this stage. The difference is in the allocation of marks: in N5 there are 4 marks for comparing the given poem to one of your choice, whereas in Higher there are 6 marks for comparing the given poem to one of your choice.

  N5 • 4 marks are given for references to another poem.

  o There is 1 mark for reference and 1 mark for comment, which means you need to make two references and one basic comment for each reference.

  H • 6 marks are given for references to another poem or poems, with all marks dependent on the quality of your comments.

  o There are 0 marks for reference and 1 mark for analytical comment, which means you need to make six references and six basic (but analytical) comments.

  o Or you can give three references with more insightful or developed analyses (which gain 2 marks each).

Sample 8- and 10-mark questions

By referring to *In Mrs Tilscher's Class* and at least one other poem, show how the poet uses imagery effectively to convey themes.

By referring to *War Photographer* and at least one other poem, show how Duffy explores painful experiences.

By referring to *Mrs Midas* and at least one other poem, show how Duffy presents dramatic characters.

By referring to *Originally* and at least one other poem, show how Duffy conveys change as a feature of her poetry.

By referring to *The Way My Mother Speaks* and at least one other poem, show how Duffy explores the nature of relationships in her poetry.

By referring to *Valentine* and at least one other poem, show how Duffy uses contrast effectively to convey theme.

N5 This section illustrates how to answer the sort of questions asked in the exam. In each case turn to the poem using the page reference given. There are two questions per poem. Each question is followed by some commentary on how to answer the question and then there are possible answers, with the awarding of marks indicated in brackets. The answers are not exhaustive – other answers are also possible.

Mrs Midas (pages 6 and 10)

1 Read verses 1 and 2.

By referring to two examples of language, explain how the writer creates a change in tone between these verses. **4**

Comment

Tone questions are usually best answered by word choice. Verse 1 creates a relaxed tone, whereas verse 2 has a more threatening tone, anticipating the problems that are to come. Consider words or expressions that create these two tones.

For example, in verse 1: 'late September' suggests a time associated with golden colours and mellow evenings; 'relaxed' suggests the speaker is stress-free, unperturbed; 'poured a glass of wine' suggests her daily chores are over, a time for leisure and repose; 'gently' suggests unhurriedly. There are other examples, but these are sufficient to answer the question.

In verse 2, the change in tone is created by 'visibility poor', 'dark', 'drink the light of the sky', the enjambement 'the way / the dark of the ground' places emphasis on 'the dark of the ground', suggesting threat, something foreboding.

Possible answers

Verse 1

- 'relaxed' (1) suggests that the speaker is stress-free, at ease (1)
- 'gently' (1) suggests unhurried, lightly (1)

Verse 2

- 'visibility poor' (1) suggests that she can't see clearly, suggesting things are becoming obscure (1)
- 'dark' (1) suggests threat, uncertainty (1)

2 Look at lines 37–43.

By referring to two examples of language, explain how the writer makes it clear that their relationship has deteriorated. **4**

Comment

To show that the relationship has deteriorated, you have to show what it was like before and how it is now. Again, word choice is perhaps the best way to answer it. She says that they 'were passionate *then*' – that is, in the past, but that now they have 'Separate beds' and he is 'below', meaning that not only are they no longer sleeping together but they sleep on different floors, which is a measure of the extent to which their relationship has deteriorated.

Possible answers

- 'You see, we were passionate then' (1) suggests that in the past they had a close, emotionally vibrant relationship (1)

- 'Separate beds' and the fact that his room is now 'below' (1) suggest that not only are they no longer sleeping together but they sleep on different floors (1)

Valentine (page 14)

1 Read lines 6–10.

By referring to two examples of word choice, explain how the writer creates a strong sense of danger. **4**

Comment

Duffy uses various words and expressions to convey a sense of danger: the minor single-word sentence 'Here' can be read as a dismissive, almost blunt tone, suggesting that the giver is in control and doesn't want her gift rejected; the word 'blind' suggests that love is out of our control, and, combined with 'with tears', suggests that we can be very hurt by love or left heart-broken if we are rejected; 'a wobbling photo of grief' makes clear that love can bring tears and heartache.

Possible answers

- 'blind' (1) suggests that people are blinded by love and it can be out of our control (1)

- 'with tears' (1) suggests that love can make us feel hopeless and desperate (1)

2 Read lines 18–20.

By referring to two examples of language, explain how the writer makes clear the speaker's idea of love. **4**

Comment

The imperative (command) 'Take it' makes clear that the speaker's lover has not yet accepted the onion; the tone is more than dismissive – it is domineering, not at all romantic; the image 'Its platinum loops shrink to a wedding ring' is a metaphor comparing the colour of an onion's rings to the colour of a platinum wedding ring, while the image 'shrink' suggests reduction, implying that there is something diminutive about marriage, that it creates constraint, restrictions on freedom, and is emotionally limiting; 'if you like' is a throwaway remark, suggesting a casual proposal – if you fancy it.

Possible answers

- 'Take it' (1) suggests that the speaker's lover has not yet accepted the onion; the tone is not at all romantic (1)

- 'shrink' (1) suggests reduction in size as well as suggesting that marriage limits relationships, especially emotionally (1)

In Mrs Tilscher's Class (page 18)

1 Look at lines 17–23.

By referring to two examples of imagery, show how the writer conveys the changes taking place throughout the Easter term. **4**

Comment

The question is about imagery, therefore you need to be able to identify the images that Duffy uses: the metaphor of 'inky tadpoles' changing from 'commas into exclamation marks'. The word 'inky' is comparing the colour of the tadpoles to the black colour of ink and 'commas into exclamation marks' now compares the change in shape and size of the tadpoles from small and comma-shaped to the much larger shape of an exclamation mark, indicating the growth of the tadpoles but also the growth of the children.

Possible answers

- the metaphor 'inky tadpoles' (1) compares the colour of tadpoles to classroom ink, capturing their black colour (1)

- 'changed / from commas into exclamation marks' (1) compares the growth of the tadpoles to the change from a comma to an exclamation mark, suggesting that throughout the Easter term they grew significantly (1)

2 Look at lines 24–30.

Using your own words as far as possible, explain two important ideas explored in the final verse. **2**

Comment

Because it is a 'use your own words' question, there is no need for quotation or reference; however, if you find it easier to answer the question using a quotation, you can still do so, but be aware you will not gain marks for the reference. There are several ideas explored in this verse: clearly summer and the end of term has arrived; the pupils are growing up and excited; the persona is braver in asking Mrs Tilscher awkward questions – the persona knew that the question about how she was born was awkward; it was time for end-of-school reports; they were keen to leave; they were already on the verge of tumultuous adolescence.

Possible answers

- it was the end of term and the beginning of the summer holidays (1)
- the pupils were eager to leave primary school (1)

Originally (page 22)

1 Read lines 4–8.

By referring to two examples of language, explain how the writer makes clear that the children were unhappy about moving home. **4**

Comment

There are examples of word choice which convey the children's unhappiness: 'My brothers cried' – their tears convey their distress; 'bawling' can be used as a measure of just how almost hysterical one of them was at the prospect of moving away; the list – 'as the miles rushed back to the city, / the street, the house, the vacant rooms / where we didn't live any more' – suggests the journey in reverse, looking back at where they used to stay, a measure of their reluctance to go forward; the speaker says that she 'stared / at the eyes of a blind toy, holding its paw' – suggesting her quiet apprehension, looking for comfort.

Possible answers

- 'bawling' (1) suggests that one of the brothers was nearly hysterical at moving home (1)

- 'stared / at the eyes of a blind toy' (1) suggests that she was quietly apprehensive, looking for comfort from her familiar toy (1)

2 Look at lines 9–12 (down to '… accent wrong').

Explain any two important ideas conveyed in these lines. **2**

Comment

There are three important ideas in these lines: (i) all childhood involves moving from one stage to another as we grow up; (ii) some changes take time to develop; (iii) some changes take place very quickly. You don't need to give references but do so if you think they will help you answer the question, but remember that there are 0 marks available for quotation.

Possible answers

- all childhood involves moving from one experience to another as a measure of growing up – indicating a transition from one stage in life to another (1)

- some transitional changes take place slowly, such as feeling isolated when you've gone to somewhere new (1)

The Way My Mother Speaks (page 26)

1 Read lines 1–5.

By referring to two examples of imagery, explain how the writer conveys the
speaker's anxiety in this verse.   **4**

Comment

There are two images in this verse: 'shallows of my breath' suggests either that she is
speaking low so that no one in the train can hear her or that she is speaking low to
herself – in either case it implies she is anxious; 'restful shapes moving' could suggest
several things: it isn't the shapes that are 'restful' but the shapes in her mind that are
moving, the inside of the train is restful while the scenery moves or vice versa; together
the contrasting images 'restful' and 'moving' imply her anxiousness.

Possible answers

- 'shallows of my breath' (1) suggests that she is speaking low so that no one in the train can
  hear her or that she is speaking low to herself, implying that she is anxious (1)

- 'restful shapes moving' (1) – it isn't the shapes that are 'restful' but the shapes in
  her mind that are moving, implying a lack of restfulness, so together 'restful shapes
  moving' implies her anxiousness (1)

2 Read lines 23–24.

Explain how these lines make an effective conclusion to the poem.   **2**

Comment

Questions about the conclusion require you to pick an expression from the designated lines
and show how they refer back either to an expression or an idea mentioned earlier.

Possible answers

- The word 'homesick' (1) refers to the earlier idea in verse 1 that she is missing her
  mother, suggested by the fact that she repeats over and over the mother's phrases (1)

- the word 'free' (1) refers to the idea that she is travelling south for new experiences (1)

- 'in love / with the way my mother speaks' (1) refers back to the title of the poem (1)

War Photographer (page 30)

1 Look at lines 1–6.

Identify two things that we learn about the war photographer from the first verse. **2**

Comment

This is an 'identify' question: all you have to do is make two points about the war photographer. Underline any two aspects that you can find: for example, we know that he is 'finally alone' – but there is no need to comment, just state that fact. We know that he takes his job very seriously because he is compared to a priest. You can use references if it helps you answer the question, but there are 0 marks for quotation. Use your own words where possible.

Possible answers

- he is on his own at last when he enters the dark room (1)
- he takes his job very seriously (1)

2 Look at lines 13–18.

By referring to two examples of language, explain how the writer conveys the photographer's emotions at this point in the poem. **2**

Comment

It is best to answer such a question using word choice. It is important to recognise that you are asked about his emotions, not about what is happening. The first indication of his emotional reactions when home is the emerging developing photograph, when the stranger's features 'faintly start to twist before his eyes' followed by 'a half-formed ghost' – where 'twist' suggests that he feels knotted discomfort inside him as the photograph appears before him, and 'half-formed ghost' suggests that he sees the ghost of the dead man he photographed now in his head, almost haunting him. There are also expressions such as 'the cries / of this man's wife' which suggests the impact of the memory on him, and 'blood stained ... dust', the horror of which has clearly distressed him.

Possible answers

- 'twist' (1) suggests that the image emerging from the developing photograph causes him painful upset as he sees the man in agony (1)
- the word 'cries' (1) conveys how intensely he still hears the distraught man's wife (1)

Higher Exam-Style Questions

H This section illustrates how to answer the sort of questions asked in the exam. In each case turn to the poem using the page reference given. There are two questions per poem. Each question is followed by some commentary on how to answer the question and then there are possible answers, with the awarding of marks indicated in brackets. The answers are not exhaustive – other answers are also possible.

Mrs Midas (pages 6 and 10)

1 Look at verses 1 and 2.

By referring to at least two examples of language, analyse how the writer creates a change in tone between these verses.   **4**

Comment

Tone questions are usually best answered by word choice and/or imagery. Verse 1 creates a relaxed tone, whereas verse 2 has a more threatening tone, anticipating the problems that are to come. Consider words or expressions that create these two tones.

For example, in verse 1: 'late September' suggests a time associated with golden colours and mellow evenings; 'relaxed' suggests the speaker is stress-free, unperturbed; 'poured a glass of wine' suggests her daily chores are over, a time for leisure and repose; 'gently' suggests unhurriedly. The use of personification in 'The kitchen / filled with the smell of itself' suggests that the kitchen was alive, but relaxed in a self-satisfied way. There is further personification in 'steamy breath / gently blanching the windows', again suggesting that the kitchen breathes, its breath condensing on the windows, an image of calm in contrast to the disturbing events that are to come. The simile – Mrs Midas 'wiped the other's glass like a brow' – suggests a slow movement; however, wiping someone's brow suggests that all is not well with them, thus anticipating the problems to come.

In verse 2, the change in tone is created by 'visibility poor', 'dark', 'drink the light of the sky', the enjambement 'the way / the dark of the ground' places emphasis on 'the dark of the ground', all suggesting not only a lack of clarity ahead, but also 'dark' connotes threat, danger to come.

You can choose to answer the question using four examples, with basic comments, each worth 1 mark, or you can use two examples, each with a more detailed comment worth 2 marks (that is, 1 + 1 + 1 + 1 or 1 + 1 + 2 or 2 + 2). You must give a reference but it is not worth any marks.

Possible answers

Verse 1

- 'relaxed' suggests that the speaker is stress-free, at ease (1)
- 'gently' suggests unhurried, lightly (1)
- 'late September' suggests a time associated with golden colours and cooler, misty, mellow evenings, all suggesting an unhurried time of day and year (2)

Verse 2

- 'visibility poor' suggests that she can't see clearly, that things are becoming obscure (1)
- 'dark' suggests threat, uncertainty (1)
- the use of enjambement – 'the way / the dark of the ground' – emphasises 'the dark of the ground' on the new line, suggesting not only a lack of clarity ahead but also 'dark' connotes threat, danger to come (2)

2 Look at verse 5.

By referring to at least two examples, analyse how the writer's use of language creates an impression of Mrs Midas' character. **4**

Comment

An impression of any character is created by language – word choice, sentence structure, imagery. The question can be answered using both word choice and sentence structure. For all 4 marks, it is possible to give four examples of word choice with related, straightforward comment and analysis, but you could also gain all 4 marks by giving two references with more developed comment and analysis. There are plenty of references that create an impression of Mrs Midas at this stage: 'I started to scream', 'I finished the wine', 'on my own', 'hearing him out', 'I made him sit', 'on the other side of the room', 'keep his hands to himself', 'I locked the cat in the cellar', 'I moved the phone', 'The toilet I didn't mind', 'I couldn't believe my ears'. All of these expressions are relevant and appropriate for an answer, but other language devices are considered in the answers below.

Possible answers

- 'I started to scream' suggests that Mrs Midas is suddenly frightened, maybe even inclined to panic, at what she sees as scary situations (1)
- the enjambement 'I finished the wine / on my own' suggests a change in her attitude, that she can be quick to recover and practical enough to finish the wine, and also by spilling 'on my own' over onto the next line, the reader is taken aback – not only is she capable of calmly finishing the wine, but she does so 'on her own' without thinking of her husband, suggesting that she is capable of being self-centred, even in a crisis (2)
- 'The toilet I didn't mind' – the short declarative sentence adds humour by suggesting that despite her anxieties, Mrs Midas' pretentiousness is always near the surface – she rather likes the idea of a gold toilet (1)

Valentine (page 14)

1 Read lines 6–10.

By referring to at least two examples of language, analyse how the writer creates a strong sense of the adverse aspects of love. **4**

Comment

Duffy uses various words and expressions to convey a sense of threat: the minor single-word sentence 'Here.' can be read as a dismissive, almost blunt tone, suggesting that the giver is in control and doesn't want her gift rejected; the word 'blind' suggests that love is out of our control (Eros and Cupid, the Greek and Roman gods of love, respectively, are depicted as blind), and, combined with 'with tears', suggests that we can be very hurt by love or left heart-broken if we are rejected; 'a wobbling photo of grief' – an image of the lover having been hurt and/or rejected – makes clear that love can bring tears and heartache; the word 'grief' connotes the misery felt when people lose someone they love.

Possible answers

- 'Here.' – because of its position, attention is drawn to this single-line, single-word minor sentence, emphasising its dismissive, almost blunt tone, suggesting that the giver is in control and doesn't want her gift rejected. On the other hand, this word could be read as the speaker's unconcerned attitude since she doesn't rate gifts very highly (2)

- the word 'blind' suggests that people have no control over those with whom they fall in love, implying that love can be unforeseen and random, but it also suggests that love is beyond our control; the phrase 'blind you with tears' further suggests that we can be very hurt by love or left heart-broken if we are rejected (2)

2 Read lines 18–23.

By referring to at least two examples of language, explain how the writer makes clear the speaker's attitude to her relationship with her lover. **4**

Comment

The imperative (command) 'Take it' makes clear that the speaker's lover has not yet accepted the onion; the tone is more than dismissive – it is domineering, not at all romantic. The image 'Its platinum loops shrink to a wedding ring' is a metaphor comparing the colour of an onion's rings to the colour of a platinum wedding ring, while the image 'shrink' suggests reduction, implying that there is something diminutive about marriage, that it creates constraint, restrictions on freedom, and is emotionally limiting; 'if you like' is a throwaway remark, suggesting her proposal can be accepted – or not – but it is not up for discussion. The single-line, single-word minor sentence – 'Lethal' – is threatening, making clear that the speaker thinks that love can be destructive. The idea of 'scent' clinging suggests that, like the scent of an onion, love can't be easily got rid of; the repetition of 'cling' suggests that the speaker doesn't approve of or want someone who is demanding and dependent; ending on the word 'knife' makes clear that she can cut the relationship at any time.

Possible answers

- the imperative 'Take it' makes clear that the speaker's lover has not yet accepted the onion – the tone is now almost domineering, not at all romantic (1)
- 'Its platinum loops shrink to a wedding ring' is a metaphor comparing the colour of an onion's rings to the colour of a platinum wedding ring, while the image 'shrink' suggests reduction, implying that there is something diminutive about marriage – that it creates constraint, restrictions on freedom and is emotionally limiting (2)
- the single-line, single-word minor sentence – 'Lethal' – is threatening, making clear that the speaker thinks that love can be destructive (1)

In Mrs Tilscher's Class (page 18)

1 Look at lines 17–23.

By referring to at least two examples of imagery, analyse how the writer conveys the changes taking place throughout the Easter term. **4**

Comment

Duffy uses the metaphor of 'inky tadpoles' changing from 'commas into exclamation marks'. The word 'inky' is comparing the colour of the tadpoles to the black colour of ink and 'commas into exclamation marks' now compares the change in shape and size of the tadpoles from small and comma-shaped to the much larger shape of an exclamation mark, indicating the growth of the tadpoles but also the growth of the children. The use of the sound image 'croaking' adds humour to the picture of the 'line of kids' following the released frogs – not only does the word suggest that the children are imitating the noise of the frogs, but it also suggests that their voices are beginning to break.

Possible answers

- the metaphor – 'commas into exclamation marks' – compares the change in the tadpoles from small and comma-shaped at the beginning of the Easter term to the much larger shape of an exclamation mark towards the end of the term, indicating the growth of the tadpoles but also the growth of the children (2)
- the sound image 'croaking' adds humour to the picture of the 'line of kids' following the released frogs; the word suggests that the children are imitating the noise of the frogs, but it also suggests that their voices are beginning to break (2)

2 Read lines 29–30.

Evaluate the effectiveness of these lines as a conclusion to the poem. **2**

Comment

Refer to aspects of these two lines – especially language – to show how they make an effective conclusion. For example: 'You ran through the gates' makes clear that it is the end of the school session and therefore the end of the poem; 'Reports were handed out' also suggests the conclusion of the year and therefore of the poem; 'impatient to be grown' suggests the anticipation of new experiences and therefore the conclusion of old ones; 'sky split open into a thunderstorm' is highly dramatic and therefore a memorable way in which to conclude the poem.

Possible answers

- 'You ran through the gates' makes clear that it is the end of the school session and therefore the end of the poem (1)
- 'impatient to be grown' suggests the anticipation of new experiences and therefore the conclusion of old ones (1)

Originally (page 22)

1 Read lines 1–3.

Analyse how effective these lines are as an opening to the poem. **2**

Comment

Look for ways in which the lines introduce the subject matter of the poem: 'came from our own country' introduces the idea of moving from one country to another; 'in a red room' suggests the inside of the transport taking them to their new house, with 'red' signifying a warning of troubles ahead; 'which fell through the fields' supports the idea of a journey south to England; 'our mother singing' introduces the idea of family and also suggests that she is trying to perk up the dispirited children; the internal para-rhyme of 'fields' and 'wheels' creates a rhythm that is appealing to a reader.

Possible answers

- 'came from our own country' introduces the subject matter – the idea of moving from one country to another (1)
- 'our mother singing' introduces the idea of family and also suggests that she is trying to perk up the dispirited children (1)

2 Read lines 15–16.

Analyse the effectiveness of the writer's use of imagery in these lines. **2**

Comment

There is only one image in these lines – the simile 'stirred like a loose tooth'; it suggests that just as a loose tooth is constantly irritating because we can't help prodding at it, so her worries about her parents' concerns are constantly with her, irritating her.

Answer

- the simile 'stirred like a loose tooth' – just as a loose tooth is constantly irritating, so her worries about her parents' concerns are constantly with her, irritating her (2)

The Way My Mother Speaks (page 26)

1 Read lines 1–5.

By referring to at least two examples of language, analyse how the writer conveys the speaker's anxiety in this verse. **4**

Comment

You can answer this referring to imagery or to rhythm. The image 'shallows of my breath' suggests either that she is speaking low so that no one in the train can hear her or that she is speaking low to herself – in either case it implies she is anxious. The oxymoron 'restful shapes moving' suggests the underlying idea that for her the shapes are both 'restful' and 'moving', either physically (the inside of the train is tranquil while the scenery appears to move or vice versa) or mentally (her thoughts are both tranquil and racing). The repetition of '*The day and ever*' has a rhythm that reflects the rhythm of the train, reminding her that the train is taking her away from the closeness of her relationship with her mother, contributing to her feelings of anxiety.

Possible answers

- 'shallows of my breath' suggests that either she is speaking low so that no one in the train can hear her or that she is speaking low to herself, implying that she is anxious (2)

- in the oxymoron – 'restful shapes moving' – the apparent contradiction reveals the underlying idea that for her the shapes are both 'restful' and 'moving', either physically (the inside of the train is tranquil while the scenery appears to move or vice versa) or mentally (her thoughts are both tranquil and racing), both of which are a measure of her anxiety (2)

2 Read lines 6–9.

Analyse how the poet uses language to convey her feelings at this point in the poem. **2**

Comment

Duffy uses transferred epithet – 'slow evening' (it isn't the evening that is slow but the train journey) – which also suggests that she feels that everything is too slow. The personification – 'the slow evening / goes down England' – suggests not only a journey south but also the word 'down' has connotations of being downhearted. The expression 'browsing for the right sky' suggests that she is looking for the right experience, while 'sky' along with 'too blue' represents her happiness at home and 'cool grey' represents her apprehension at experiences to come.

Possible answers

- the transferred epithet – 'slow evening' (it isn't the evening that is slow but the train journey) – suggests that she feels that everything is too slow, indicating that she is a little impatient (2)

- 'browsing for the right sky' suggests that she is looking or hoping for the right experience, while 'sky' along with 'too blue' represents her happiness at home and 'cool grey' represents her apprehension at experiences to come (2)

War Photographer (page 30)

 Look at lines 13–18.

By referring to at least two examples of language, explain how the writer conveys the photographer's emotions at this point in the poem. **4**

Comment

You are asked about the photographer's emotions, not about what is happening. The first indication of his emotional reactions when home is the emerging developing photograph – when the stranger's features 'faintly start to twist before his eyes' followed by 'a half-formed ghost': the word 'twist' suggests that he feels knotted discomfort inside him as the photograph appears before him, and 'half-formed ghost' suggests that he sees the ghost in his head of the dead man he photographed, almost haunting him. There are also expressions such as 'the cries / of this man's wife', suggesting the impact of the memory on him, and 'blood stained … dust', the horror of which has clearly distressed him. In the enjambement – 'He remembers the cries / of this man's wife' – the run-on 'of this man's wife' highlights his memory of the sheer agony felt by the wife for the dead man. Conflicting emotions are suggested by 'sought approval' – he is a professional photographer who earns his salary by taking the most provocative war photographs, yet in this instance he feels morally obliged to ask the wife's permission to take the photograph. The climactic position of 'foreign dust' creates a powerful image that echoes 'ashes to ashes, dust to dust', developing his earlier priest-like image as compassionate yet disturbed by what he saw.

Possible answers

- 'faintly start to twist before his eyes' followed by 'a half-formed ghost': the image refers to the emerging photographic image of the dying man; the word 'twist' suggests that he feels knotted discomfort inside him as the photograph appears before him, and 'half-formed ghost' suggests that he sees the ghost in his head of the dead man he photographed, almost haunting him (2)

- the enjambement – 'He remembers the cries / of this man's wife', where the run-on 'of this man's wife' highlights his consciousness of the sheer agony felt by the wife for the dead man, and 'cries' reveals his memory of her pain at her husband's death – shows he is sensitive to the suffering of others and feels their pain (2)

2 Read lines 19–24.

By referring to at least two examples of language, analyse how Duffy creates a bitter tone. **4**

Comment

Duffy uses contrast to suggest tone: the expression 'A hundred agonies' – indicating the huge number of photographs he has taken to expose the utter cruelty of war – is contrasted with 'his editor will pick out five or six', a sign of the editor's lack of concern about the suffering; the editor is interested only in the shock value of the photographs. There is also the contrast between the readers' short-lived, minimal reaction to the photographs ('eyeballs prick / with tears') and the 'hundred agonies' of the war victims; 'bath and pre-lunch beers' also creates a contrast between what the photographs depict and the readers' comfortable, carefree lives. These contrasts create the bitter tone.

Possible answers

- 'a hundred agonies' – indicating the huge number of photographs taken, all revealing the utter cruelty of war – is contrasted with 'his editor will pick out five or six', a sign of the editor's lack of concern about the suffering; the editor is interested only in the shock value of the photographs (2)

- the contrast between the readers' short-lived, minimal reaction to the photographs ('eyeballs prick / with tears') and the victims' 'hundred agonies', while 'bath and pre-lunch beers' also creates a contrast between what the photographs depict and the readers' comfortable, carefree lives, making a bitter comment on complacency in the UK (2)

The Way My Mother Speaks

I say her phrases to myself
in my head
or under the shallows of my breath,
restful shapes moving.

5   *The day and ever. The day and ever.*

The train this slow evening
goes down England
browsing for the right sky,
too blue swapped for a cool grey.

10   For miles I have been saying
What like is it
the way I say things when I think.
Nothing is silent. Nothing is not silent.
What like is it.

15   Only tonight
I am happy and sad
like a child
who stood at the end of summer
and dipped a net

20   in a green, erotic pond. *The day*
and ever. The day and ever.
I am homesick, free, in love
with the way my mother speaks.

N5 Questions

1. Identify, in the first four lines of the poem, two main ideas of the poem. 2

2. By referring to lines 6–9, show how two examples of the writer's use of language suggest the speaker's feelings at this stage in her journey. 4

3. In lines 15–20, explain how the writer's use of simile clarifies her ideas. 4

4. How effective do you find the final two lines as a conclusion to the poem? 2

5. By referring to this poem and at least one other by Duffy, show how the poet conveys the nature of change. 8

H Questions

1. Look at lines 1–4.
   Analyse how imagery is used to convey the speaker's feelings. 2

2. Look at lines 10–14.
   By referring to at least two examples, analyse how the use of poetic technique conveys the speaker's affection for her mother. 4

3. Look at lines 15–20.
   By referring to at least two examples, analyse how language is used to convey the speaker's lack of certainty. 4

4. By referring to this poem and at least one other by Duffy, show how the poet conveys the nature of relationships. 10

Glossary

Adjective – a word that describes a noun.

Alliteration/alliterative – repetition of the same consonants, usually to highlight what is being said.

Antanaclasis – repetition of the same word with differing meanings.

Antithesis – direct opposite.

Assonance – repetition of similar vowel sounds to create rhyme or to highlight (usually the tone) what is being said.

Audial – related to sound or hearing.

Autobiography – a book written by an author about himself/herself.

Clause – a unit of sense below the level of a sentence.

Cliché – an overused expression, lacking in originality.

Climax – a significant or dramatic final point.

Colloquial – language of everyday speech.

Conjunction – a word that joins together or connects other words, phrases, clauses (but, and, or).

Connotation – whatever a word suggests (rather than means).

Connote – suggest.

Contradiction – a combination of two terms that oppose each other.

Contrast – two ideas, words or images that appear opposite or very different but which together reveal an underlying significance.

Couplet/rhyming couplet – two successive lines of verse which rhyme.

Declarative (sentence) – a sentence which makes an assertion or gives information in a definite way.

Double entendre – a word or phrase capable of being interpreted in two ways.

Double negative – a phrase containing two negative elements, which can be used for emphasis to stress the negative or could cancel each other out to suggest a positive.

Dramatic – relating to drama – striking, exciting.

Dramatic monologue – a poem told in the first person, in which the speaker reveals aspects of their character.

End-stopped (line) – the natural break at the end of a line of poetry, created usually by a punctuation mark.

Enjambement – when sentence structure takes priority over line structure.

First-person narration – where a character or speaker uses 'I' or 'me'.

Free verse – verse which has no regular rhythm or rhyme.

Guttural – sound made at the back of the throat.

Hackneyed – overused expression, devoid of significant meaning.

Humour – words or phrases which amuse in order to make a point.

Hyperbole – the use of exaggeration for heightened effect.

Image/imagery – mental picture of an idea or object.

Imperative – the part of a verb that expresses a command.

Internal rhyme – rhyming words within lines of poetry.

Irony/ironical – stating the opposite of what is meant to make a significant point.

Italic – a cursive font (*italic*).

Juxtaposition – the placing of words, images or ideas side by side.

Kinetic (energy) – describing anything in terms of movement.

Kitsch – poor taste, too sentimental or brash.

Liquid – (sound effect) the 'l' sound.

List – series of items usually separated by commas or by conjunctions.

Literal – the explicit meaning of a word.

Metaphor – a device of comparison, saying one thing is something else.

Minor (one-word) sentence – a sentence without a main verb.

Monosyllable – word of one syllable.

Onomatopoeia – using a word which sounds the same as the sound of the thing it names.

Oxymoron – words or ideas that appear to be contradictions.

Paradox – words, phrases, images or ideas that seem to contradict each other.

Para-rhyme – a half rhyme, a rhyme which isn't quite pure.

Parenthetical/parentheses – an expression that is additional to a sentence yet grammatically independent, usually signalled by pairs of brackets or dashes but sometimes commas.

Paronomasia/paronomastic – a pun on words, usually for humorous effect.

Pejorative – the tone of a word that suggests disapproval or unpleasantness.

Persona – the speaker in a poem.

Personification – ascribing human qualities to inanimate objects.

Perspective – point of view.

Plosive – the hard 'b' and 'p' sounds.

Polysyndeton – the placing of conjunctions (and, or, nor, but) between each item in a list to intensify the point being made.

Reductive – making an idea overly simple.

Refrain – repeated lines, usually at the end of a verse.

Repetition – words, phrases or expressions repeated for emphasis or dramatic effect.

Rhetorical question – a question that implies its own answer.

Rhyme – words with the same or similar vowel sounds, often at the end of lines of poetry.

Rhyme scheme – the pattern of sounds used at the end of lines of poetry, usually indicated by lower case letters (e.g. *a a b b* or *a b b a*).

Rhythm – a repeated pattern of stressed sound, although the repetition does not have to be regular.

Semantic field – words which are related in meaning.

Setting – the place or time in which an event takes place.

Sibilant – the soft 's', 'z' sounds.

Simile – a device of comparison, saying one thing is like something else.

Sound image – a mental representation of a sound.

Stereotype – a fixed or simplified idea about what someone or something is like using a set of characteristics (accent, dress, hair style).

Symbolism/symbol – the use of an object to represent something else.

Synaesthesia – one sense being perceived as another.

Synecdoche – where a part of something is used to represent the whole.

Tense – the use of verbs to indicate time (present – *I jump*; past – *I jumped*; future – *I shall jump*).

Third-person (narration) – where the reader is addressed by someone not part of the narrative, using 'he', 'she' or 'they'.

Tone – the feeling of a piece of writing that conveys the writer's attitude to the subject matter.

Transferred epithet – where an adjective associated with a person is used to describe an inanimate object.

Tricolon – a list of three items, a rhetorical device that is climactically effective.

Verse paragraph – where one verse leads on from the previous verse while exploring a different aspect of content.

Word choice – a word or words used for their connotative meaning and effect.

Answers

Note that the following answers are not exhaustive; they show possible answers and indicate the allocation of marks (e.g. (1)).

Pages 6–9, *Mrs Midas* 1

- N5 • 'I served up the meal' (1) suggests quiet mealtime domesticity (1) whereas 'spitting out the teeth of the rich' (1) suggests a sudden change with Midas' gift having turned corn to gold (1)

- • 'He toyed with his spoon' (1) – he enjoys turning cutlery into gold which contrasts with 'I poured with shaking hand' (1), conveying her nervousness at what was happening (1)

- H • the final line – 'as he picked up the glass, goblet, golden chalice, drank' – shows the dramatic transformation of his glass to a golden chalice, with the latter's connotations of poison (2)

- • the theatrical transformation is reinforced by the alliteration of the ugly guttural 'g' sound, suggesting the drama of everything turning to gold (2)

Pages 10–13, *Mrs Midas* 2

- N5 • 'So he had to move out' (1) presents her as in control (1)

- • 'under cover of dark' (1) shows that she has become embarrassed by his presence (1)

- H • the short declarative sentence 'So he had to move out' shows she was determined to be rid of him and that she can be decisive and controlling when she has to be (2)

- • 'the woman who married the fool / who wished for gold' reveals her as annoyed and frustrated at what she sees as her husband's stupidity; 'fool who wished for gold' reveals that she isn't materialistic – her values are different from his – she doesn't like what he wants in life (2)

Pages 14–17, *Valentine*

- N5 • 'as we are, / for as long as we are' (1) suggests that their love will go on for as long as it lasts and no longer (1)

- H • 'Its fierce kiss' – the transferred epithet makes clear that it is the kisser who is being fierce, which isn't necessarily an indication of love; it suggests that the kiss is about domination and control, which won't necessarily last (2)

Pages 18–21, *In Mrs Tilscher's Class*

- N5 • 'This was better than home' (1) – she finds the classroom more exciting than being at home (1)

- • 'Coloured shapes' (1) – the minor sentence emphasises the decorated appearance of the classroom (1)

- H • in lines 10–11, the use of the short sentences, especially the three minor sentences ('Enthralling books', 'Sugar paper', 'Coloured shapes') gives snapshot images of the classroom as well as an impression of the activities that took place – reading, crafts (2)

- • the simile 'like a sweetshop' compares the classroom to the excitement and colour of a sweetshop, conveying how attractive it was to the speaker; it also suggests the mouth-watering sense of anticipation felt by children as they look at an array of sweets (2)

Pages 22–25, *Originally*

- N5 • 'My brothers cried' (1) – suggests that they were very young; 'one of them bawling' (1) suggests that one of them was very young (1)

- H • 'in a red room' – the metaphor suggests that from a child's perspective the interior of a car appears as large as a room, while 'which fell through the fields' again from a child's perspective suggests that the car is heading south, going 'down' the way (2)

- 'I stared / at the eyes of a blind toy' suggests that because the toy has lost an eye it has been in her possession for a while; and word choice 'staring' suggests that she is slightly anxious, frightened even, and can't look elsewhere (2)

Pages 26–29, *The Way My Mother Speaks*

N5 • the repetition of '*What like is it*' (1) makes clear that her mother's saying is going over and over in her head, revealing her apprehension at going somewhere new (1)

H • 'browsing for the right sky' suggests that, although the train is the subject grammatically, the personification makes it clear that it is the persona who is browsing 'for the right sky', that is, looking for something appropriate and better, but 'browsing' suggests her uncertainty, not sure what she is looking for (2)

- 'too blue swapped for a cool grey' suggests that she is leaving her attractive life behind and venturing into the unknown, slightly depressing future (1)

- 'Nothing is silent. Nothing is not silent' – the double negative in the second sentence and the juxtaposition of the two sentences reinforce her feelings of confusion (1)

Pages 30–33, *War Photographer*

N5 • 'he is finally alone' (1) – the use of 'finally' suggests that he has wanted to be alone for some time, suggesting his need to be solitary, in order to have peace and be serious (1)

- 'as though this were a church' (1) – churches are renowned for being serious places, so he takes his dark room seriously (1)

H • the semantic field of churches – 'only light is red' suggests dark room light as well as church altar light – makes clear how serious he is towards his work (1); 'as though this were a church' and 'he / a priest' suggests the seriousness with which he takes his job (1); the minor sentences 'Belfast. Beirut. Phnom Penh' emphasise the war-torn cities (1), something the photographer takes seriously, further highlighted by the plosives, which add to the noise and violence, again a measure of serious warfare (1)

Pages 36–37, Time

- in *Originally* and *In Mrs Tilscher's Class*, Duffy uses first-person narration, recounting the speaker's personal experience set in time; both poems begin with the past (leaving Scotland and the beginning of her last year at primary school) and take the reader through progressive stages, ending with a reflection on the nature of the experience

- in *The Way My Mother Speaks,* she uses the train journey beginning in the evening and ending with thoughts about her future destination

- in *Mrs Midas* and *Valentine*, Duffy uses dramatic monologue to reveal the character of the speaker, but also to suggest time; in *Mrs Midas*, time is used to show how the events affect her relationship – beginning in domestic relaxation and ending in regret; in *Valentine*, time is used by setting the poem in the present ('I give you an onion') but ends in future prediction – love/the scent of the onion 'will cling to your fingers / cling to your knife'

- in *War Photographer*, the past in the war zones affects his attitude to the complacency of the public in the UK

Answers

Pages 38–39, Conflict

- in *Mrs Midas*, she conveys conflict between the warm relationship Mrs Midas and her husband used to have – 'we were passionate then', 'halcyon days' – and their separation now – 'Separate beds', she 'put a chair against [her] door' while he was in the 'spare room'. There is conflict and ultimate incompatibility between her values of warmth and a loving relationship and the value he places on wealth (gold)

- in *Originally*, the conflict between the move from Scotland to England is expressed by the children's reactions – the behaviour of the brothers and her emotional withdrawal by holding her toy. There is conflict between the uncertainty of their immediate reactions to the new place and their subsequent acceptance

- the conflict in *The Way My Mother Speaks* is largely internal, expressed subtly by 'restful shapes moving' and 'happy and sad' and 'homesick, free'. There is conflict in the way the speaker symbolises her past life with her mother as the 'right sky' and the future as 'cool grey'

Pages 40–41, Nature of Relationships

- in *Valentine*, the speaker rejects stereotypical, romantic relationships represented by the commercialism of Valentine's Day, stating that conventional relationships cannot be guaranteed to last. She suggests that relationships can be based on possessiveness and fidelity and that such aspects of relationships do not

necessarily last forever. She suggests that relationships based on love can be dangerous, even deadly

- in *War Photographer*, the main relationship is between the war photographer and his work, although the nature of this relationship is complex: his attitude is professional when in war zones, but emotional and aware of suffering when developing his photographs at home. His relationship with his editor is bitter; 'the reader's eyeballs prick / with tears between the bath and pre-lunch beers' shows his frustration that his readers' concern is limited and temporary

Pages 44–45, Sound Effects
Valentine

- the two central lines of the poem – 'I am trying to be truthful' and 'Not a cute card or a kissogram' – both use alliteration. In the first, the alliteration of the 't' sound draws attention to her desire to be honest by its use in 'trying' and 'truthful'. In the second, the alliteration of the guttural draws attention to the tawdry gifts peddled on Valentine's Day

Pages 46–47, Enjambement
The Way My Mother Speaks

- in lines 20–21 in particular, the sentence '*The day / and ever*' runs on, thereby creating a gap at the end of the line that perhaps replicates a jolt in the movement of the train, while at the same time emphasising 'and ever', perhaps highlighting the length of the journey and suggesting the phrase in her head, repeated over and over

Pages 48–49, Imagery: Comparison
Valentine

- the central image is the metaphor of the onion – it is not only a surprising gift for a lover on Valentine's Day but also suggests a comparison with love: just as an onion is in layers so love can be peeled back to expose all that is entailed, a relationship can be stripped of its layers to expose what it really is composed of

Pages 50–51, Imagery: Representation and Contrast

In Mrs Tilscher's Class

- Representation: 'skittle of milk' represents childhood innocence; 'window opened with a long pole' represents the increasing heat of the morning; 'inky tadpoles' represents the use of classroom ink as well as nature study

- Contrast: 'Brady and Hindley' contrasts with the security and love within the classroom

Pages 52–53, Rhythm and Sentence Structure

In Mrs Tilscher's Class

- in verse 2, Duffy opens the verse with a declarative short sentence: 'This was better than home', stating unambiguously that she preferred being in Mrs Tilscher's class to home

- the minor sentence – 'Enthralling books' – draws attention to what must have been one of the speaker's main interests – books

- after another short sentence drawing attention to the simile – 'like a sweetshop' – there are two more minor sentences, the effect of which is to snapshot the amount of art materials to be seen

Pages 72–73, Practice Exam

1
- the speaker keeps repeating her mother's phrases in her head (1)

- she says them under her breath so that no one will hear her (1)

2
- 'slow evening' (1) suggests that the speaker feels impatient with the slowness of the train journey (1)

- 'browsing' (1) suggests that she is travelling to look for new experiences or opportunities (1)

3
- the simile 'like a child' (1) clarifies her ideas because although she is leaving home (1) she is uncertain (1) in a way that a child would be apprehensive about embarking on anything new (1)

OR

- the simile 'like a child' (1) clarifies her ideas because she realises that her confusion of happiness and sadness is child-like, even immature (1) because she is leaving the happiness of her homelife (1) to embark on experiences yet unknown (1)

4
- 'the way my mother speaks' (1) recalls the title of the poem (1)

5   *Commonality*

- *The Way My Mother Speaks* deals with the change of the speaker moving away from home for the first time. The speaker conveys the idea of moving from the love of her mother and the security of her home by means of the train journey metaphor. In *Originally*, Duffy also conveys the nature of change by using the experience of moving to the family's new house (2)

Given poem

- 'I am homesick, free' (1) suggests that the speaker is confused by the change – she misses her home greatly, yet knows that her new life will not have the constraints of the old (1)

Originally

- 'But then you forget' (1) – the speaker has forgotten her old life as she adjusts to the change of moving home (1)

- 'my tongue / shedding its skin like a snake' (1) – the simile makes clear that she loses her previous accent as she adjusts to the change (1)

H 1
- 'restful shapes moving' – the apparent contradiction in the oxymoron conveys two possible ideas concerning the speaker's confusion about moving away from home: (i) the scenery seems to move as the train moves but the inside of the

Answers

carriage is still; (ii) her thoughts are agitated yet at the same time they appear to her to be quite still – all suggesting her confused feelings (2)

2 • she has been repeating the mother's phrase – 'What like is it' – 'for miles', an indication of the extent of her mother's influence on her; also, the rhythm of the phrase, reinforced by the repetition, replicates the steady rhythm of the train and reinforces the sense of her mother's influence on her (2)

   • 'Nothing is silent. Nothing is not silent' – the alliteration of the nasal 'n' sound and the repetition of 'nothing' and the use of 'not', along with the double negative in the second sentence, all reinforce the apparent contradiction of noise and the lack of it, again contributing to her mind's unrest as she misses her mother – she hears her silently surrounded by the noise of the train (2)

3 • the expression – 'Only tonight / I am happy and sad' – is one of many apparent contradictions conveying the speaker's confused state about moving from home – she is happy at the prospect of a new life but sad at leaving behind her mother's love (2)

   • 'stood at the end of summer' suggests that she is at the end of a warmly loving part of her life, her home and the closeness of her relationship with her mother; the 'end of summer' implies the arrival of autumn and ultimately winter, the latter two seasons representing chills to come – the use of the seasons helps convey her lack of confidence (2)

4 *Commonality*
   • Duffy conveys the nature of relationships in both *The Way My Mother Speaks* and *Mrs Midas*. The former depicts the speaker's loving relationship with her mother; the latter begins with a relaxed relationship that ends because of Mrs Midas' experience of her husband's greed. Both poems use symbolism to portray the nature of relationships (2)

Given poem
   • the position of 'the right sky' at the end of the line reinforces its symbolic significance: the sky represents the state of her life and 'too blue' in the next line suggests that it has been almost too perfect and happy, and is to be 'swapped' for 'a cool grey', suggesting that life could become icy, distant and colourless (2)

Mrs Midas
   • 'Separate beds' symbolises the fact that they no longer sleep together and that therefore their relationship has deteriorated because her husband's 'gift' turns all he touches into gold; the result of his 'gift' is further made clear by the fact that they don't just have separate beds, they now live on separate floors (2); that he is 'turning the spare room / into the tomb of Tutankhamun' shows his golden touch, which is causing the separation in their relationship, and the idea of 'tomb' symbolises the death of their life together (2)

   • Mrs Midas' regret at the ending of their relationship is symbolised by the 'bowl of apples', the sight of which 'stopped [her] dead': we can infer (work out) that the apples were Golden Delicious, which, along with 'certain lights, dawn, late afternoon' are all golden colours, reminding her of her husband and their former happy relationship (2)